What people are saying about
The Facilitative Way:

"*The Facilitative Way* is based on nearly 20 years of research done by the Institute of Cultural Affairs between the mid-1950s and the mid-1970s. By interpreting the language of the ICA the authors have made these models and methods of social change accessible to a broad range of business men and women concerned about the human factor in organizational change."

> — Jon C. Jenkins, Author, *International Facilitator's Companion*, Imaginal Training, Groningen, The Netherlands

"*The Facilitative Way* is not simply a "how-to" manual. It gives in-depth background and context as well as comprehensive screens and charts to help effectively negotiate the complex ambiguity in organizations that we all sense is there. *The Facilitative Way* does an excellent job of translating ICA's (the Institute of Cultural Affairs) theoretical work into some very practical organizational applications. Managers in corporate, non-profit or governmental situations will find new and helpful approaches to the problems we all face."

> — Bob Vance, Past President, International Association of Facilitators; President, Strategics International Inc., Miami, Florida

"This is must reading if you care about people and assisting them in getting the necessary work done quickly and well. With shrinking dollars and more expected of everyone, we need to be able to work together to accomplish the work. The information offered in this book is the kind we can use to get the job done well. As a supervisor, I am more in tune now with listening to what others have to say and encouraging them by asking questions rather than offering solutions. It has made my job a lot easier and more rewarding. Finally, a self-help manual for those of us who want to make a difference in the workplace."

> – Marilyn Kurtz, Economic and Employment
> Support Supervisor, Kansas City Area Office of
> Social and Rehabilitation Services, State of Kansas

"Wilson makes the case for facilitative leadership from three perspectives – the 'why' it is needed today, the results that flow from it, and the 'how to do it.' Simple but powerful, her reflective, facilitative and strategic models are illustrated with engaging vignettes from her years of working with teams. This blend of stimulating ideas and practical advice illustrates the richness and wholeness that can occur within teams led by a facilitative leader. Wilson gives us a stimulating and refreshing guide for becoming the facilitative leaders this new century demands of us."

> – Patricia Tuecke, President, Sierra Circle
> Consulting, Reno, Nevada

"*The Facilitative Way* simplifies the complexity of dynamic organizational structures and applies years of documented research to real-life business challenges. TeamTech's workshop approach provides the perfect balance of information, applied learning and hands-on action. The Dynamics Screen is a "must have tool" for leaders today, and *The Facilitative Way* is the optimum tool box."

> – Donna S. Byers, Senior Vice President,
>   Direct Services, American Century Investment
>   Services, Inc., Kansas City, Missouri

"I very much like the 'facilitative capacity' approach laid out in the introduction. The use of stories throughout the book is terrific. They are engaging and provide a useful context for the ideas that are presented. The explanation of practical methods (e.g., Dynamics, FFID, Workshop Method) is useful."

> – Sandor P. Schuman, Editor, *Group Facilitation:*
>   *A Research and Applications Journal,* Moderator,
>   The Electronic Discussion of Group Facilitation,
>   Albany, New York

"*The Facilitative Way* uses real-life stories and situations as examples of how good management can elevate your organization. In my personal experience of working with the authors, I have never worked with people who did a better job of keeping us energized and focused on our goals. This book is full of creative and energetic ways to change how you think, how you act, and how you lead."

> – Gordon Docking, Chief Executive Officer,
>   St. Mary's Hospital, Blue Springs, Missouri

The Facilitative Way

Leadership That Makes
the Difference

The Facilitative Way

Leadership
That Makes
the Difference

Priscilla H. Wilson

Kathleen Harnish and Joel Wright

teamtech
enabling people to think together

TeamTech Press
Shawnee Mission, KS

The Facilitative Way
Leadership That Makes the Difference

Copyright © 2003, TeamTech Inc.

www.teamtechinc.com

Book cover and interior design by Tim Lynch

Book publishing services by BookWorks Publishing, Marketing, Consulting

Publisher's Cataloging-in-Publication

Wilson, Priscilla H.
    The facilitative way : leadership that makes the
difference / Priscilla H. Wilson, Kathleen Harnish, Joel Wright.
        p. cm.
    Includes bibliographical references and index.
    LCCN 2003092044
    ISBN 0-9729764-0-X

    1. Leadership. 2. Group facilitation. I. Harnish, Kathleen.
    II. Wright, Joel, 1939- III. Title.

HD57.7.W55 2003   658.4'092
QBI03-200326

The Facilitative Way is dedicated to the memory of
Evelyn Mathews Edwards and Joseph Wesley Mathews.
Through their commitment and dedication, the
facilitative way was opened for us.

Acknowledgments

There are many people to whom I owe a debt of gratitude. A special thanks to my partners, Kathleen Harnish and Joel Wright, for their support and access to the materials we corporately produced on which this book is based. The intellectual capital of the Institute of Cultural Affairs is the foundational base that has made *The Facilitative Way* possible. My thanks to the many ICA colleagues who have shared their knowledge with us.

In addition, input and feedback from many people has kept this project on the straight and narrow with creative suggestions. I wish to particularly thank Kaze Gadway, who helped me frame the book's initial outline. A special thank you also to Maggie Finefrock, Marnie Hammer, Marilyn Kurtz, Wayne Nelson, Barbara O'Hearne and Dave Skinner for their invaluable feedback.

The gratitude I have for the assistance and insights of Pola Firestone of BookWorks as she guided this effort to final publication is immeasurable. Editing assistance from B-J Diamond, Deborah Shouse and Kirsten McBride has been invaluable.

Above all, I am deeply grateful for my husband Rodney's encouragement, support and patience.

Priscilla H. Wilson

Contents

Generate Reflection

Ignite Action

Capture Learning

Introduction

Leading is a decision, not a job description.

In the early 1990s, a large city hospital asked our consulting company, TeamTech, to teach a group of managers "some communication skills." Communication issues topped the list of major issues in many organizations at the time. After the communication skills training we worked with several hospital departments that were experiencing conflict and controversy. What started with a simple request for communication skills training moved to a wider scope of organizational concerns. Eventually, this broadened to facilitation training for managers and supervisors in all of the hospital's departments. Over time, more and more clients requested facilitation training for people who were in various leadership positions – managers, supervisors, team leaders and so on.

Working with people in business, government and the community over many years has taught us that the capacity to be facilitative is at the core of working effectively with others. People who are facilitative catalysts help colleagues work together smarter, faster and more comfortably with enthusiasm and fun. The facilitative process fosters ownership, teamwork, better communication overall and results. As one manager said, "After practicing this for several months, I've found that people around me are adopting the same techniques. We accomplish more in shorter amounts of time, we trust each other more and we are more open with each other. We collaborate and celebrate in coming up with solutions that are much better than if we'd worked on things on our own."

The Facilitative Way, which is based on the facilitation training we typically offer, was written for those who are in positions of responsibility for individuals, teams, tasks and their organization: non-profit, governmental or for-profit. *The Facilitative Way* examines the skills, techniques and methods needed to help people think and act together to make a difference. This book can help you think, talk and act cooperatively when you use effective combinations of reflective, facilitative and strategic processes.

The insights and processes presented here are based on international research of the Institute of Cultural Affairs and the insights of Dr. W. Edwards Deming. Priscilla and Joel were in leadership and board positions with the ICA for twenty years and helped in the development of many of the ICA methods.

Kathleen served in a one-year internship with Dr. W. Edwards Deming, one of the world's best known advocates in the quality movement of the 1970s and 1980s. For over thirty years we have seen the power of disciplined reflection and have watched people express ideas about how to make things work better. We have observed meaning and purpose reenter a situation and seen spirit and fulfillment motivate people. We have heard individuals make sense out of their complex situations. Many of the stories in this book reflect this spirit and sense of fulfillment. Our insights are drawn from a long and varied history of working with groups of people from rural villages to corporate boardrooms.

The Facilitative Way offers new ways to achieve a "people" emphasis and create a supportive atmosphere to express innovative ideas. "Being facilitative" means easing the work processes for yourself and others by thinking together. "Thinking strategically" means taking into account the whole as well as the necessary details to make strategic choices that accomplish desired outcomes.

Changes in the marketplace and the necessity to give service demand a more facilitative and strategic workplace. Today's information-based economy with its high customer demands and global competition is requiring a new level of speed, imagination and flexibility, affecting every aspect of our work life. This need for speed, imagination and flexibility is causing many of the changes in today's workplace. These changes in turn are calling for an increase in people skills, such as:

Change – upgrade your thinking skills

What you know is important; but how you think, make decisions and act is critical. It is important to upgrade your thinking skills at the same pace as you upgrade your RAM and megabytes. Don't find yourself with Version 1 thinking in a world operating on Version 6.0. The workplace has shifted from "brawn" to "brains" as we all struggle to let go of old assumptions of the industrial economy.

Change – work effectively together

Increasingly, jobs emphasize both technical responsibility and people responsibility. Too often when the nurse has been promoted to unit supervisor or the bank teller to branch manager, they lack the necessary people skills for their new responsibilities.

Change – talk with people, not at them

Leaders need to understand how to use the resources and people that surround them. You can be a leader without being the official "manager" or "project lead." It's not about telling others what you know, it's about listening more actively and being sure that everyone involved has made a contribution.

Change – think with a big-picture perspective

Leaders need to adopt big-picture thinking so that all the dynamics at play in a problem can be identified and a strategic response developed.

Change – choose to take responsibility

Responsible action is the goal, and individual choice is the vehicle. When responsible thinking is released, people are fully engaged and get things done.

Throughout *The Facilitative Way* we will share tools and techniques for being strategically facilitative and responding more effectively to situations, problems and issues. The key is in the together as we strive to work with new modes of thinking and acting. Making interactions easier starts with each of us.

Through tools, theory, procedures, reflections and thinkabouts you will learn how to take advantage of the research that has been done on the teaching of thinking. Watch for the following icons found throughout the book to guide your learning.

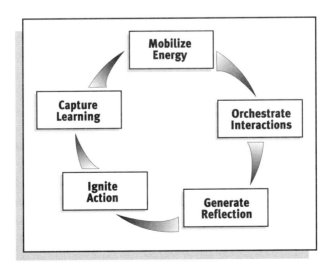

Learning Flowchart

At the beginning of each facilitative approach chapter is a flowchart delineating the key points of the chapter. This enables you to see the logical flow of what you are learning.

The Facilitative Approach

Key understanding of the aproach and method covered in that arena.

Reflection

Questions to help you and others think about thinking. These questions deepen learning and increase your ability to apply learning

Thinkabouts

Information and understandings that add depth to implementing the method.

How-to Action

Practical ways to use the methods and tools in work situations.

When you learn, practice and apply the facilitative models presented here, you will be more effective at:

- Analyzing what a given situation requires
- Raising the questions that make a difference
- Getting more impact with less energy
- Generating buy-in for what is needed
- Engaging people in thinking and taking action together

Decide to be a facilitative leader, and others will think of you as a person who knows how to get things done with others.

Make a Difference

Strive for 100 Percent Engagement

Choose to be a leader!! Who me? That's right. At one point in time – not so long ago – leaders were designated, assigned, specified.

In today's marketplace of global competition, constant change and expanding customer choice, being a leader is something you choose to be (or not to be) right where you are. If customers (internal or external) are going to receive the service that they expect, it is up to you to step up to the bat.

When Harry Truman was president of the United States, we were not surprised when he put on his desk a sign that read, "The Buck Stops Here." What would your workplace be like if every person had a sign that read, "The Buck Stops Here"? What would it be like if there was 100 percent engagement?

The Gallup Organization regularly surveys the U.S. workforce to measure levels of employee engagement. "The latest figures show that only 30 percent of the U.S. workforce consists of engaged employees (loyal and productive). Over half – 54 percent – are not-engaged (just putting in time), while 16 percent are actively disengaged (unhappy and spreading their discontent)."[1]

Why is such a high percentage of the workforce not engaged? Is it because old forms of security and certainty have disappeared and we haven't figured out how to operate standing on a bowl of Jell-O? Regardless, we all may be in need of new tools and processes to increase active engagement.

Reflective Learning

Where do you find yourself in this survey:
- engaged?
- not-engaged?
- actively disengaged?

What about individuals you work with, your team, your department?

Perhaps you are fortunate and engagement levels are high in your workplace. But if not, have you thought about how to change things to reach 100 percent engagement?

Too often we think that more supervision, salary increases, higher status or better relationships in the workplace are the motivators for engagement. According to Frederick Herzberg[2] in "One more time: How do you motivate employees?," these are "hygiene" or job satisfaction factors. But the factors, he says, that lead to extreme employee satisfaction or motivation for engagement are:
- achievement (receiving feedback that includes praise and recognition)
- the work itself
- responsibility (participating in communication, accountability, self-scheduling)
- advancement and growth (receiving new learning and unique expertise)

In these changing times new leadership strengths and interconnections between people and events are necessary to engage employees. "No society on the planet knows how to live with constant, radical change. It's never been done before," says William Van Wishard, president, WorldTrends Research.[3]

Create a New Context for Working Together

**Change is now the norm. We are caught between the
no longer and the not yet.**

We have moved out of an industrial age and are overwhelmed by the information age. We struggle to make sense of it all. The to-do list never gets shorter and never gets done. How-to books are plentiful, and many suggest ways for you to do your job better. You need ways for you and your coworkers to learn how to think, talk and take action together. These skills are at the heart of facilitative leadership.

"Shared commitment to change develops only with collective capability to build shared aspirations. People start discussing 'undiscussable' subjects only when they develop the reflection and inquiry skills that enable them to talk openly about complex, conflictive issues without invoking defensiveness," according to Peter Senge.[4] The facilitative skills that support this collective capability lead to more involved engagement.

Being facilitative is a different way of interacting with coworkers and viewing a task. According to *Webster's Dictionary*, "facilitate," from the root word "facile," is to "make easy or easier." It means functioning with a mindset of serving others, allowing the group and the situation to "be in control." As a manager, this emphasis on people skills is powerful. Instead of having to "know," you need to build the capacity for more people to "be in the know."

Facilitative leaders are engaged in:
- Asking questions to enrich engagement
- Sharing knowledge and information
- Linking minds
- Learning and unlearning

Ask Questions to Enrich Engagement

Norma Jean is looking for ideas on how her team can make more informed decisions. As a project leader in a large global asset management firm, she knows that her team members often have trouble remembering verbal instructions. She hopes to expand her skills so that communication in the team will improve. She is searching for ways to help projects move forward more efficiently and effectively.

The most poignant "Ah Ha" moment for her during a training class on facilitative skills is when Norma Jean realizes that leaders and managers don't have to have all the answers themselves. When she hears the trainers and the class participants talking about how to use the resources and people that are in the group, she knows she has just learned a new way to think about her role with the team.

The facilitative way means shifting from "keeping control" to new ways of asking questions and relating to people so they can assume more responsibility. Helping a group of people face its challenges lets them build a clear picture of the situation so they move on actions.

Jeffrey Pfeffer and Robert Sutton[5] state in a *Harvard Business Review* article that "most organizations have trouble bridging the knowing-doing (talk-action) gap ... because of the willingness to let talk substitute for action." Further, they reaffirm that "leaders who do the work, rather than just talk about it, help prevent the knowing-doing gap from opening in the first place."

> *Howard had just been in a training class that emphasized the importance of developing team ownership for a project. He decided to try out the concepts at his next team meeting and created a list of questions to keep the ideas rolling.*
>
> *After setting up the brainstorming session, Howard launched in with the first question. He waited for ideas to pour out of people, but, instead, the team just looked at him. Howard chewed on his lip, anxiously waiting. Finally, Jane came up with an idea.*
>
> *"Good," Howard said, writing it down. "By the way, this reminds me of another idea. We should really do ...," and he wrote down his own idea as well. Then Fred suggested something else and Howard wrote that down too. "I've had an experience with an idea like that back when I was working on ... The idea reminds me of this idea ..."*
>
> *Every time a team member had an idea, Howard had an idea. He was so excited by the wealth of his own ideas that he didn't seem to notice the room growing quieter and quieter. Taking over with his own ideas instead of listening to and honoring the team's brainstorm had effectively shut down the creativity of the group.*

Peter Drucker[6] says that "managing yourself requires taking responsibility for relationships ... taking responsibility for communication. People do not know what other people are doing and how they do their work, or what contribution the other people are concentrating on and what results they expect. And the reason they do not know is that they have not asked and therefore have not been told."

Share Knowledge and Information

John is sent to a training class to gain a new skill, to learn a new way of doing things. John comes back from training with new DOING but no new THINKING skills. He quickly gets busy and with time of the essence, John's same thinking kicks in. Soon he even falls back into the old doing rather than new doing. How can you get John to start THINKING about what he is DOING?

Thinking in new ways is hard, but it is a necessity in today's knowledge-based economy.

What we carry in our heads and share with others is what gets the job done: intellectual capital, knowledge work and intangible assets of skill, knowledge and information.

Without sharing and accumulating knowledge and learning, businesses keep "losing the recipe," as hard-earned learning walks out the door when people change jobs or are let go.

Link Minds

The complexity and speed of change have made it impossible for one person to know it all. Issues are too complex for a simple "one size fits all" approach. Therefore, linking minds in order to think, talk and take action is critical. Everything is more connected, complex and diverse. Just one for instance: communication technologies have shifted our linkages. When a major shift takes place in the workplace, rumors fly between the people not in the communication loop, resulting in confusion and mixed messages.

When we think together, we can focus critical skills on real work situations. As a result, work gets done and practical learning happens. We have to understand what we collectively carry in our heads. The concepts we pull together corporately about making the right things happen are key to getting tasks completed.

Thinking together can be hard work. Since our work life may consume 25-40 percent of our week, it is helpful to make this chunk of time more effective and enjoyable. Without collective thinking on a problem:
- cynicism spreads
- people get disgruntled
- turnover increases
- burnout spreads
- things don't get done
- the things that can make a difference don't happen

Learn and Unlearn

If you still think you are supposed to be making all the decisions, you will not be successful in learning how to be facilitative. Effective leadership requires learning and unlearning. Training often centers on learning and applying new skills, ignoring the unlearning that must take place first. *Fortune* magazine noted: "Companies expect middle managers to metamorphose, effective yesterday, into leaders ready to coach, motivate and empower. The problem is, few managers and companies understand the transformational process. Corporations underestimate the shift in mindset and behavioral skills that team leaders need."[7]

Learning together can spark intrinsic motivation for employee achievement, recognition, involvement, role clarity, responsibility, advancement, growth, empowerment and results.

Shift from Facilitator to Facilitative

If we are to keep from boiling over, we have to step back and think (reflect) in order to learn new ways of producing results. This need to learn together is causing a major shift in our working together.

The First Wave

In the first wave of encouraging participation and engagement, the role of facilitator was created. This role grew out of the quality circles created as a result of the work of Dr. W. Edwards Deming in the 1950s in Japan, and from 1974 until his death in 1993 in the United States. The facilitator was responsible for orchestrating the process and helping a group achieve a desired outcome. The quality management movement pointed out the need for this role and popularized it. "Being facilitative" typically referred to the individual specifically assigned to manage the group process, as in:

"All right, now on this team we need a leader, recorder and facilitator."
"The facilitator is the one concerned with the process."
"Let's bring in an outside facilitator for this retreat."
"We need someone to facilitate this event."

The Second Wave

The surf was up, as the second wave of "being facilitative" moved beyond an assigned role. We began to see that many people – not just one in a group or team – can decide and learn to be facilitative. This involves using a style of behavior that eases the way people think and take action together. The role of assigned facilitator evolved to becoming instrumental in showing others how to be more facilitative in their day-to-day work.

A Transformational Wave

A third wave is beginning to sweep the workplace. This wave combines being facilitative with being strategic and calls for facilitative leadership throughout an organization. Working together facilitatively and strategically means that thinking and action are tied to the organization's strategy, mission and vision and the capacity of people to carry it out.

When working strategically, a group's thinking and planning stays connected to:
- the historic – what has happened in the past in the organization and industry?
    - what was the original passion/plan?
    - what have been benchmarks along the way?
- the present – what is going on now?
    - what is the current mission/message?
    - what are current accomplishments?
- the future – what is needed and what are the priorities for the future?

In the third wave, being facilitative and strategic means asking the right questions and carrying out the strategic action. It sounds simple, but being facilitative, at its most fundamental level, is about changing your relationship with people and the relationship people have to the job.

Being facilitative rests on the premise of talking with, not at, people. In fact, in empowered teams everyone acts in a facilitative role.

Figure 1 shows the differences between a facilitative and a nonfacilitative approach.

Differences Between a Facilitative and a Nonfacilitative Approach

Facilitative Approach	Nonfacilitative Approach
• dialoguing along with giving a report	• giving a report
• asking open-ended questions	• talking at people
• sparking new thinking	• controlling the conversation
• linking ideas together	• isolating individual thinking
• sparking motivation and passion	• giving instructions
• acknowledging everyone	• paying attention only to the important people
• moving a group to action	• processing forever

Figure 1

The art and science of facilitation continues to evolve. Taking time to master facilitative skills and operate strategically can catalyze effectiveness in a complex, changing environment. Energy and enthusiasm will transform the working environment.

What It Means to Be "Facilitative"

Now we recognize the need for everyone to be adept at easing the way for people to think and take action together in a variety of interactions (from meetings to conversations) and in a variety of organizational roles (manager, customer service rep, team member, CEO).

Being facilitative starts with a decision to work together to achieve an outcome. It does not necessarily mean that everyone is involved in every decision. Being facilitative may mean asking for input for a decision that you need to make; a decision may be delegated to one or more people; or a decision may be made with the information available at the time.

Facilitative people:
- discern relevant patterns
- spot issues and options
- think comprehensively
- generate passion for the task
- operate with a stance of possibility
- reinforce esprit de corps

You are being facilitative when:
- you make a decision and then help others understand the decision and why it is needed so they can more effectively implement it.
- you ask people for their input and insights with the clear understanding that the ultimate decision is yours.
- you explain the criteria for an acceptable decision and turn the decision over to others, providing them with the responsibility and accountability necessary to get it done.

Know Your Way Around

It Starts with You

Anyone can decide to ease the conversation and work on behalf of the team. Team members, coworkers, managers, supervisors, team leaders or frontline workers can be facilitative. Facilitative skills can enhance participation in a meeting, a conversation in the hall, an informal discussion at lunch, a presentation or a workshop.

Do you make it easier for yourself and others to get the task done?
Do you help groups get unstuck?
Do you encourage dialogue and keep action happening?

Reflective Learning

When you think in terms of group ideas, do you:
- tap into everyone's useful reservoir of thinking?
- pay attention to each person's ideas?
- affirm each person's contribution?
- honor the unique gifts of each individual?

9

- give people a sense of "we are in this together"?
- build on the ideas of the group to create something new?

Work Smarter

The art and science of working with others allows us to work smarter, not harder. According to David Perkins, getting smarter is a matter of "knowing your way around" different situations.[8]

You are probably already familiar with many of the challenging places you need to "know your way around," for instance:

- decision-making – choosing between alternatives
- problem-solving – building bridges across the gaps
- explanation – finding insight and meaning
- problem finding – seeking and addressing potential flaws and weaknesses
- planning – formulating plans and organizing and allocating resources
- prediction – conceptualizing existing or known conditions to forecast likely outcome
- learning – integrating new information, concepts and skills

Knowing your way around facilitative leadership can make the difference in the interactions in your workplace. Figure 2 shows the new thinking and the new doing that are the result of knowing your way around facilitative leadership.

Take the BE–THINK–DO Journey

Deciding to be facilitative and strategic in the workplace is a journey that consists of many facets. First and foremost, it is a journey of learning about yourself, others and the task. It is a journey of risk, and therefore requires courage. It is a journey of building relationships. Finally, it is a journey of increasing capacity to get things done.

This journey changes your approach. You will decide to BE the hub of a wheel, not a tire(d) repair shop; you will THINK through perceptions in new ways; and you will DO the methods and techniques that win, rather than those that circle around, ultimately going nowhere.

This BE–THINK–DO journey gives you a facilitative advantage at the individual, team and organizational level.

Knowing Your Way Around

Facilitative Approach	The New Thinking	The New Doing
Mobilize Energy with the Dynamics Screen	*Comprehensive thinking* with organizational dynamics	Use leverage to inform strategic action
Orchestrate Interactions with an intentional script	*Intentional thinking* in advance about what needs to happen	Shape a team environment
Generate Reflection with a sequencing formula	*Facilitative thinking* that taps into people's natural thinking process	Focus creativity to unleash the power of multiple perspectives
Ignite Action with vision-reality tension	*Enthusiastic thinking* that harnesses the creative tension to make strategic choices	Strategically allocate the use of time, energy and resources
Capture Learning with a compelling story	*Reflective learning,* unlearning and relearning	Reenergize, remaneuver and sustain strategic action

Figure 2

Advantages for you as an individual:
- You don't need to have all the answers.
- You interact with coworkers and superiors with more confidence.
- You can take risks with courage by thinking through how to make things happen.
- You experience ways in which you can make a difference.
- You have more fun on the job.

Advantages for the team or work group:
- A team finds ways to move beyond an often confusing collection of individual opinions to reach a common understanding of a given task.
- A team feels confident in moving beyond discussion to action.
- A team both gives and receives feedback.
- A team saves time getting things done by thinking together before acting.
- A team discovers the joy of working together to reach a goal by working smarter, not harder.

Advantages for the organization:
- Teams handle disputes and conflicts.
- Teams build collegial, inclusive relationships with customers and coworkers.
- People share a common purpose and know how to strengthen it.
- Effectiveness becomes the norm in handling change.
- Feedback moves up, down and across, constantly informing and improving teams and the organization.

Snowball Effect

To enhance this BE–THINK–DO journey, adopt an operating style that eases the way for people to think and take action together. As a result, others will start using these skills as well:
- instead of one facilitator at the head of the table, everybody around the table is facilitating the group process;
- instead of a person complaining, "why don't they do something," those around the table pick up responsibility;
- instead of one loud voice dominating the team, those around the table share insights.

Summary

The changing workplace in today's information age makes facilitative leadership skills essential. By easing the way for conversations, by building active and empowered teams, by showing people the benefits of thinking and acting together, you create a better work life for yourself, your team and your organization. It starts with your decision to expand a mix of techniques, skills and approaches that will make working together more effective and satisfying.

Mobilize Energy

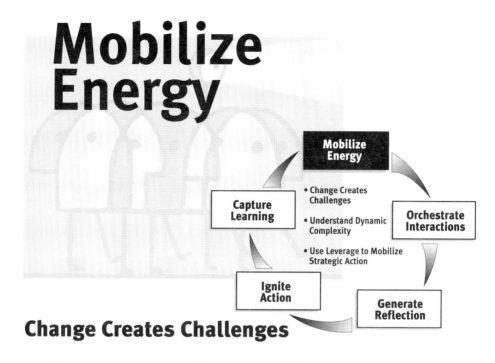

- **Mobilize Energy**
  - Change Creates Challenges
  - Understand Dynamic Complexity
  - Use Leverage to Mobilize Strategic Action
- Orchestrate Interactions
- Generate Reflection
- Ignite Action
- Capture Learning

Change Creates Challenges

Change comes at us faster than we can assimilate it, resulting in a temptation to hang on to the security of defined tasks in isolated departments as traditionally has been the case. Below are three examples of the struggles we face when we fear we will not know what to do when things change.

Do More With Less

- *The Situation: Larry's team is working on a computer project when two members are transferred to another department. Larry realizes that no new members will be transferred in, and with fewer people there is still the same amount of work to do. The team is faced with: Do more with less.*

  The Choices: The team can work harder and simply reassign the work the two transferred members were doing. Or they can invent a new mode of organizing the project. Or they can reprioritize their work and come back to the computer project later.

  The Challenge: The team faces the challenge of starting over in fresh and creative ways. Redesigning the work will mean deciding what they need to start doing, stop doing, keep doing or do differently so they can meet deadlines.

Not Either/Or But Both/And

- *The Situation: Frida is the manager of a new team. Her question is how much participation she should encourage and how much control she should exercise. She knows it would be helpful to involve more people (get them thinking), but this runs directly into some of the controls in place (policies, procedures, standards). How will decisions be made?*

The Choices: *Frida remembers a "decision-making continuum" she learned in a training class. Maybe she doesn't have to give all decisions away or make all the decisions herself. To manage by extremes, either/or may not be the only choice. The decision-making continuum in Figure 1 allows her to have more choices.*

Decision-Making Continuum

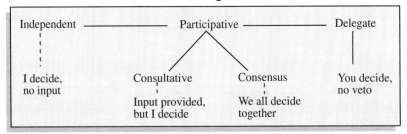

Figure 1

The Challenge: *After deciding to work with this continuum, Frida's challenge is to decide her own leadership style. Then she will need to discern which decision-making mode to use when.*

Information Is Power

- **The Situation:** *The organization's mission statement is posted in all the departments, extolling the virtues of sharing information. Yet Zachery has noticed that other managers continue to hoard information, thus broadcasting the message: Do what we say, not what we do! Zachery has trouble with the idea of hoarding information as a way of holding on to power as a manager.*

  The Choices: *Does Zachery hang on to information in order to stay in charge of the team? Does he share what he knows so people are thinking about the information and creating new perspectives?*

  The Challenge: *Zachery is challenged to find new ways to hook up information to the task so it becomes a power resource for the whole team. He wants the team to do a good job so it doesn't remain in isolation from the rest of the organization.*

Reflect on how having a bigger picture can be helpful in meeting your challenges.

- What have been some of the changes in your workplace over the last five years?
- Which changes are you experiencing as exciting and enticing?
- Which changes scare you, filling you with foreboding?
- How can you position yourself so that change doesn't tear you apart or set you drifting aimlessly.

Reflective Learning

The key to big-picture thinking in a time of complex change is understanding how things work, where they fit into the overall picture and how goals are defined and achieved. In an information economy, relationships are often the biggest challenge, and "why" is more important than "how."

Think Differently

In a stable marketplace with minimal competition and limited customer choice, the task was to just do the job, and produce consistently in the assigned spot.

Today we are facing a very different marketplace.
Extensive customer choice, vast competition and constant change
are forcing us to shift our responses.

Here's a story of how marketplace forces shape where we put our time and resources.

Imagine work life back in your grandfather's day. The typical boss made the decisions and took responsibility through bureaucratic controls, while the worker was to do his job. The purpose was to "make the numbers" and feed the marketplace. For their part, customers took whatever was made! Quantity, not quality, was the measuring stick. Whether in the auto industry, banking, retail, or even services (many fewer then), work life was pretty routine and predictable. You gave your loyalty to the company, and in return you had a secure job for life.

Sharing of information was on a need-to-know basis. Top-down leadership and decision-making were the order of the day. Work was done within structured roles; people were to stay in their box on the chart. Since the purpose was to do the job, knowledge was all about skills training. No one talked about purpose. Instead, work was done with an unspoken purpose to maximize resources.

The banks were *the* money business; for example, getting cash, making transfers and checking balances required contact with the bank during its time frame. Convenient options were not offered. The banks did not need to change their methods because no one was offering alternatives. While this meant limited choice, it provided a great deal of stability.

How different today's workplace is. The demands to meet the highly competitive, globally complex, rapidly changing marketplace have caused a shift from a "just do your job" purpose to "commit to the mission."

This shift is being driven by the need to serve customers and provide customized services. Think of your own experience as a customer. There are fifty-two places you can buy a hamburger, forty-eight places you can get your car tuned up and thirty-two places you can go for a physical check-up. As customers we are better informed, we insist on excellent quality and we want everything quickly and conveniently.

As a result of these changes, organizations are structuring more around:
- serving customers
- commiting to the mission
- building involvement

How do we give the best service to our customers and yet use our resources most wisely? The answer is: we create innovative systems.

How can we manage this? It takes all of us being fully involved in providing the quality and customer service the marketplace demands. Chris Argyris[1] describes this as employees having internal commitment, which "occurs when employees are committed to a particular project, person, or program for their own individual reasons or motivations."

The workplace still needs controls but requires a different level of support. As a result, everyone is involved in thinking and acting rather than having only the people at the "top" thinking and everyone else acting.

In today's marketplace, the "why" we do what we do has become a more critical component as we try to make sense of what is going on. We know most about "what" we need to do, less about "how" we are doing it and least about "why" it is important. There is a new push to define, communicate and live the mission and purpose of the organization. As a result, we find ourselves in much more flexible roles, doing whatever it takes, creating buy-in, producing quality.

The challenge for each of us is to create a shared picture of what we are trying to accomplish. During these changing times often the greatest struggle an organization faces is how to hold the tension between the mission statement and the bottom line.

The key is to daily find ways to make the purpose practical; for example, to think about who we are – our identity. How is your organization's identity portrayed in annual reports, press releases, quarterly statements, staff meetings, executive chats, rituals and symbols of corporate life, meeting formats, modes of speech, the way retirement dinners are conducted, symbols of recognition ceremonies, what is put on the walls?

A bureaucratic organization is not able to respond with the speed, flexibility and quality that is necessary. The question is: what capabilities do we need? How must leadership be different than in the past? Figure 2 illustrates some of the changes necessary to shift successfully from bureaucratic to facilitative leadership.

Leadership Shifts in a Marketplace of Extensive Customer Choice, Vast Competition and Constant Change

From Bureaucratic Leadership	to	Facilitative Leadership
• control		• support
• rigid		• flexibility
• job "prescriptions"		• task areas
• isolated departments		• experience of the whole
• self-interest		• common good
• focus on #s		• focus on values *and* #s
• people are cogs in a machine		• people have creative brains

Figure 2

Reflective Learning

- How are you different as a customer than your parents or grandparents used to be?
- What do you expect as an employee?
- How has your role as a manager been changing?
- What does this have to do with being facilitative?

Organizations are moving beyond bureaucratic structures, learning how to pull people together quickly from different parts of the system into effective teams working on a task. For this strategy to be effective, managers and leaders must learn how to be facilitative.

Maura was an assistant manager for a communication company. The company implemented a reorganization plan whereby project teams were created and each charged to customize their services to meet the needs of their customers (internal or external). Suddenly Maura was in charge of a team. Before, each person had worked fairly independently but now they had to come up with a plan. Some people were filled with ideas; others barely said a word. Maura couldn't figure out how to manage this group. Plus, they were getting less real work done. Morale sank and customer service was worse than before the team experiment. Maura got a knot in her stomach just thinking about work.

Finally, after a year of struggle, senior management sent out a directive to disband the teams and return to the original top-down mode of operation. Maura and almost everyone else were relieved to revert to the "I'm not paid to think" style of work. The customers, however, experienced no improvement in service. Service continued to go from bad to worse.

Reflective Learning

- What do you think was missing in the experiment with teams?
- What is the capacity of Maura's company to be flexible with change in the future?

Too often cross-functional and task-focused teams are ineffective, because they do not know how to think together and create real interdependence. Managers and employees need to know how to ease the flow of information up, down and sideways while increasing people's capacity to reflect on their own ideas. We are each called to expand our ability to develop people skills and a new sensitivity to mobilize people.

Shift Habitual Thinking Patterns

The rivers of thought carved in our minds represent habitual thinking patterns that have become ingrained. When we are under pressure, we tend to operate with an emphasis on either the Task (what has to be done), Processes (how it is to be done), or the Purpose (why we need to do it). We tend to forget the other two perspectives.

Many times our habitual ways of thinking limit our ability to see the larger perspective.

As change moves throughout the organization, so does the need for more comprehensive (task + process + purpose) thinking. This is big-picture thinking.

Figure 3 (page 20) describes three thinking perspectives, the primary concerns in each and why thinking in that perspective alone is limiting. Identify which of the three most aptly describes your own perspective. Consider your thinking when under pressure or stress in the work environment. If you have trouble identifying your favored perspective, ask a few trusted coworkers.

Once you have identified your habitual thinking mode, take a moment to reflect on:

Reflective Learning

- Which two things do you say or do that caused you to identify this as your perspective?
- What strengths/values does this perspective have?
- What are three things you can do to balance your perspective so that you are considering all aspects of a given situation?

If you lean toward the Task, broaden your thinking perspective by also considering:

- What is important?
- How will this action fit with the purpose of the team or organization?
- What information is needed to act responsibly?
- Who else needs to be involved and/or informed?

Limited Thinking Perspectives

Perspective	Primary Concern	Limitations
Focusing primarily on the <u>Task</u> **What we do**	Quantifiable and shorter term: • just do it • get to the bottom line • manage for results	Gets things done but tends to be directive
Focusing primarily on the <u>Process</u> **How we do it**	Dotting all the "i's" and crossing all the "t's:" • quicker to do it myself • detail orientation • reflection on me if not done right	Gets things done but tends to just do it oneself
Focusing primarily on the <u>Purpose</u> **Why we do it**	Making sure everyone has the same values: • why are we doing this? • have the "right" people been informed? • is our thinking long-term enough?	Gets things done but tends to try to keep everyone happy

Figure 3

If you lean toward Process, broaden your thinking perspective by also considering:

- Who are the customers and what are their needs?
- What is the purpose of this assignment?
- What's the balance between "getting it right" and "getting it done fast"?
- How does the work space need to reflect the purpose?

Finally, if you lean toward Purpose, broaden your thinking perspective by also considering:

- What are the resource constraints and financial impact?
- What systems need to be in place?
- What are the expectations?
- How does this help serve the customer?

More comprehensive thinking will broaden your perspectives and strengthen your ability to deal with unexpected change. It is easier to balance your thinking when you are not under pressure or stress. Your capacity to recognize habitual thinking modes in others can help you bring balance to a work team. When you know the different thinking modes of team members, making decisions can be strengthened by including more perspectives.

Just like people, organizations also have habitual thinking patterns or biases.

If an organization has a bias toward the Economic ...

- The bottom line is the purpose.
- Customers are valued over employees.
- The budget is the final decision.

If an organization has a bias toward the Political ...

- It tries to get everyone's say in decisions.
- There is an overemphasis on policies and procedures.
- There is either information overload or lack of information.

If an organization has a bias toward the Cultural ...

- There is a push to be nice.
- There is little emphasis on accountability.
- There is more love for the company than for the product.

Think about your team's role in the organization or a particular initiative.

- What is the primary dynamic influencing your team's role or initiative?
- What led you to your conclusion?

Reflective Learning

Abandon Old Assumptions: Adopt New Approaches

**In a marketplace that expects customized service
and is full of competition and choice, many of our long-held
assumptions are no longer true.**

We all operate with assumptions, something we take for granted and suppose to be true. The problem is that old assumptions do not change easily. As one manager put it, "Things don't change until frictional rub generates heat." Today, the "heat" is on old assumptions, and it is time to adopt some new approaches.

Rethought assumptions can move us into bold new approaches. Let's examine six workplace assumptions that are shifting.

Assumption 1
Nothing can happen without tight control on all activities. Close supervision is necessary to ensure a healthy bottom line.
New Approach
People need unblinking clarity about "why" they do what they do. Continuing conversations about compelling purpose and core values are now involving employees at all levels. New structures, processes and mechanisms that promote innovation, creativity and intrinsic motivation lead to astonishing results.

> *Our real business is solving problems. "By 1990, the mechanisms to stimulate progress at 3M had produced more than 60,000 products and more than 40 separate product divisions. The 15 percent rule is a long-standing tradition that encourages technical people to spend up to 15 percent of their time on projects of their own choosing and initiative."[2]*

> *"The key to the Post-it™ adhesive was in experimenting. If I had factored it out beforehand," said Spence Silver, the inventor of the Post-It note, "I wouldn't have done the experiment. If I had really seriously cracked the books and gone through the literature, I would have stopped." Although the invention of the Post-it note might have been somewhat accidental, the creation of the 3M environment that allowed it was anything but an accident.[3]*

Allowing employees time and space to be innovative can boost the bottom line.

Assumption 2
Workers are paid to do, not to think.
New Approach

If companies believe that their people are their most important asset, all organizational structures need to reflect that belief. All employees receive innovative training that lets them be a creative part of the action.

> *Disney's Magic Kingdom becomes a magic place not because there is "pixie dust" to make the guests (customers) feel special. Disney University's intensive training ensures the cast members (employees) have clear expectations for their daily tasks. They are trained to be performers who are always "on stage" in the theme park. This guarantees a cheerful, helpful, all-smiles, take-extra-time stance in every situation. The cast members are empowered to solve problems that the guests bring to them. All training is designed so cast members will feel like partners with the founder, Walt Disney. They perform the necessary acts to "make people happy." [4]*

Thinking workers make a difference in the level of service that customers experience.

Assumption 3
Leadership/management makes all the decisions.
New Approach

Leadership can invite everyone to assume a leadership role, adding his or her gifts and skills.

> *Open book management practiced by Springfield Remanufacturing Corporation (SRC) in Springfield, MO, gets everyone involved in making and tracking money. Their system gives employees a radically expanded role in decision-making by providing all the statistics and financial information to all employees. Open book management involves and motivates employees. Although it is hard work and you have to keep at it, the organization has better financial outcomes as employees experience being challenged by the marketplace. The responsibility for solving problems and giving customers great service is everyone's job. [5]*

Leaders at all levels of an organization need a working concept of business finances, the competitive environment and strategic thinking. The constantly changing marketplace and increasing customer demands mean that employees thinking strategically make the difference between success and failure.

Assumption 4
Narrowly defined markets and products lead to success.
New Approach

"What" we do is seldom static in winning organizations. As long as the constancy of values and purpose is focused on the process, products and services can shift with the changing demands of the marketplace.

> *Motorola struggled in its early years to find which products to manufacture and repair, but stayed constant with its proclaimed purpose of providing products and services of superior quality at a fair price. "Motorola initially entered the field of advanced electronics (transistors, semiconductors, integrated circuits) simply as a natural outgrowth of its small Phoenix laboratory set up in 1949 to develop a few electronic components for use in the company's televisions and radios. In 1955, Motorola made a conscious strategic choice to move into the electronics business in order to sell some of their output to outside customers."[6]*

Partnering with employees, customers and stakeholders to continually reinvent the next niche in the "what" has to be guided by the "why." The constancy of purpose – the why – is like the beacon of a lighthouse guiding an organization away from the shoals.

Assumption 5
The bottom line is profit.
New Approach

The bottom line is creating a committed team of customers, employees and shareholders. The profits will follow, with the triple bottom line of people, profits and the planet.

> *Patagonia made climbing hardware that advocated a more pure, equipment-light approach to the sport. Why? Because popular climbing areas were being defaced by the constant pounding of pitons, and the overuse of gear detracted from the real challenge – the climb. Climbers saw that the "lite" approach was the right thing to do. Climbers weren't carrying the weight of the pitons. Plus as one climber said, "You experience the climb as if you were making the first ascent. When you look at a crack in the rock with no scars, the esthetic of the climb is preserved." Patagonia has since taken many such stands in favor of the environment and the purity of sport, and the company continues to grow.*

Organizations grow when they pay attention to their values and allow them to shape operating decisions.

Assumption 6
People only relate to an organization for money and, unless supervised, will give less than full effort.
New Approach
People's relationships can surpass a concern for money. They want to be involved, and they want to make a difference.

> *Merck & Company elected to develop and give away Mectizan to people in the developing world who had parasitic worms swarming through body tissue. This drug cures "river blindness." For three generations Merck leadership followed ideals stating, "We are workers in industry who are genuinely inspired by the ideals of advancement of medical science, and of service to humanity." When it was clear that Mectizan in the developing world was not "profitable," rather than pull out of the market to look for profit elsewhere, Merck elected to give it away. "Asked why Merck made the Mectizan decision, Merck's chief executive pointed out that failure to go forward with the product could have demoralized Merck scientists – scientists working for a company that explicitly viewed itself as 'in the business of preserving and improving human life.'" [7]*

People want to make a difference on a global scale and are willing to share knowledge to make that difference when there is an opportunity.

- Which of your assumptions need to be challenged?

Reflective Learning

We need new ways to assess and identify which assumptions need to be challenged. When we challenge assumptions, we create an opening for change. Thinking from a systems perspective is the "make or break" of significant change. In taking into account the whole system in our thinking, we can understand the complexity of today's issues and discover more effective approaches for dealing with them.

Change Your Screen

Imagine walking into a familiar grocery store. You can picture the location of products. The milk is on the left aisle, the frozen goods in the center and the fresh vegetables and fruit are on the right. But as you walk in one day, you notice that the store has been completely rearranged. To reorient yourself, you have to redraw your mental image. You have to change your screen.

A screen is a thinking filter that helps you see and understand what is going on. It is your mental image. It helps you weed out unimportant images and focus on those that are pertinent. When you want different results, you need to "change your screen" and look at things in a new way.

- Examine the organization where you work. See if you can take in the whole picture without filters. Think of as many aspects of the organization as you can, including the dynamics at work, the interactions and processes. Look at the people as well as the products.

Reflective Learning

The organizational development department of a multidiscipline, global asset management firm employing more than 3,000 people discovered through manager surveys and departmental feedback that big-picture thinking skills were a core competency required of their employees. This competency enabled managers and their teams to be more effective when analyzing situations, anticipating implications and implementing successful decisions. They wanted employees to:
- Understand corporate decisions from a big-picture perspective
- Communicate more effectively the implications of those decisions to their departments and teams
- Make decisions using a "systems thinking" approach
- Plan and coordinate change efforts with a greater understanding of all the dynamics involved

To bring these goals about, a customized curriculum was developed and employees were trained in skills and tools to:
- Understand the major systems and structural forces at work in the

organization and how outside forces (economy, competition, technology, etc.) create pressure to change
- Utilize this learning to interpret how the company had changed over the last ten years and develop a broader understanding of corporate decision-making
- Analyze their department, team or a particular situation from a systems perspective and identify strengths, weaknesses and next steps
- Communicate clearly with employees and involve them in deciding and implementing change
- Review and plan a comprehensive approach to addressing an immediate problem or issue the employee is facing

This customized curriculum has been successful since 1996, and three managers of the asset management firm are currently teaching it four times a year. Feedback from participants on the benefits of the curriculum includes:

"It gives me a better understanding as to why my department is making some of the decisions it is in a bear market."

"I take a broader approach to making decisions."

"I am now able to better identify my role within the organization and more effectively communicate with management."

"This provides me with a structure to use when approaching problems."

"In trying to help my team through difficult times, it's a great tool for dealing with change."

The mental imagery or screen this curriculum is based on is the Dynamics Screen, which is introduced in the next section. This screen can help you frame what is needed. It will help you manage from a big-picture perspective to strategically seed innovative thinking, find entry points for action, challenge comfort zones and mobilize energy for implementation.

Understand Dynamic Complexity

"It is true that we may take a new road, operate out of a different self-image, choose another set of filters to see and respond to life."
– Basil Sharp[8]

Three Basic Dynamics

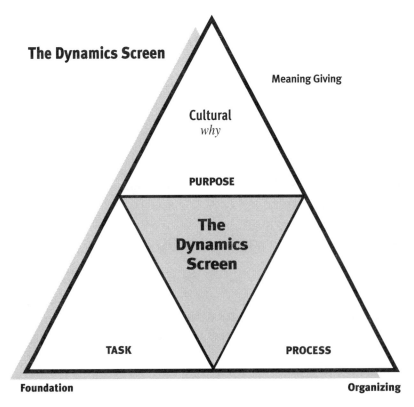

The dynamics of what we do, why we do it and how we do it in our teams, departments, organizations and even our families shape the future. Dynamics create relationships among the details. They are always present and exerting influence.

When sales drop, we ask "why?" and discover that deliveries are behind thirty days. When we ask "why?" again, we discover that the ad campaign generated a rush of orders and we couldn't keep up with the increased demand. Customers became discouraged and canceled their orders. Cause and effect are often subtly related, yet separate. The effects of decisions and actions over time are not always obvious. This is called *dynamic* complexity.

If we don't try to manage these dynamics, they will manage us. The Dynamics Screen in Figure 4 depicts the three basic dynamics of any organization

The Dynamics Screen

Meaning Giving

Cultural
why

PURPOSE

The Dynamics Screen

TASK

PROCESS

Foundation

Organizing

Figure 4

or social entity. This model can shift your thinking from a fragmented approach to a big-picture approach by letting you see patterns of behavior and relationships among the variables of tasks, processes and purpose.

There are three basic dynamics in any organized entity:

Economic Dynamic: consists of **What** the organization does. The market and the customers define the goods and/or services the organization is paid for – its foundation. Without the Economic Dynamic, there is no political or cultural reality.

Political or Social Dynamic: involves **How** the organization does what it does. The processes and procedures of doing the task – how the work is organized and how things are ordered.

Cultural Dynamic: comprises the purpose of the organization – **Why** it does what it does. This dynamic gives meaning and direction by injecting identity, values, knowledge and style into the Economic and Political Dynamics. This is the least understood dynamic because it has been the least emphasized in a time when the Economic Dynamic has been central in our thinking.

Peter Drucker states that "a theory of the business has three parts. First, there are assumptions about the environment of the organization; society and its structure, the market, the customer and technology. Second, there are assumptions about the specific mission of the organization. Third, there are assumptions about the core competencies needed to accomplish the organization's mission. The assumptions about environment define what an organization is paid for (economic dynamics). The assumptions about mission define what an organization considers to be meaningful results; in other words, they point to how it envisions itself making a difference in the economy and in the society at large (cultural dynamics). Finally, the assumptions about core competencies define where an organization must excel in order to maintain leadership (political dynamics)."[9]

"What we do," "why we do it" and "how we do it" is a common way to express the three primary dynamics. As a result, we often hear, "This is what needs to get done," "Here is how we should tackle it" or "This is why we are doing it."

We too often think "either/or," and yet we live and work in a "both/and" world. The Dynamics Screen can add to our "both/and" thinking by helping us:

- understand what is changing and why – we see the dynamics as well as the details

- understand the complexity of change – we recognize interrelationships as well as more depth in an isolated situation
- make more effective decisions – we gain leverage by thinking comprehensively as well as addressing an immediate problem

One group was using the Dynamics Screen to better understand their organization. When they first began the exercise, they felt cynical and very bottom-line oriented. They thought the only purpose of the organization was to make money. However, as they listened to each other, they began to drop their cynicism. They realized that the organization was more concerned with involving people in task forces and teams than they originally thought. As they recognized how the competitive marketplace was changing things, they got a new view of their company. The Dynamics Screen enabled them to tell stories that revealed what was actually happening as they talked through the screen with others.

"I thought our company was primarily bottom-line oriented," said one manager. "But listening to everyone else, I realize we have more values and heart than I imagined." The Dynamics Screen had made it easier to look at their tasks from more than one perspective.

- Are people in your workplace clear about "why"?
- Do things make sense?
- Is your organization employing practical change agents that will enable it to rebalance the organization?

Reflective Learning

The Dynamics Screen is a big-picture diagram used to understand the system of dynamics in which we operate. Looking at the organization through this screen can help us reorganize our thinking for more effective communication, improved distribution of products and services, organizational structure and promotion of company values.

Imagine having Level 1 of the Dynamics Screen (Figure 5) on your computer monitor. Imagine clicking on one of the three dynamics – Economic, Political or Cultural. The click opens the Level 2 triangle and you see more definition of each dynamic – the foundation, ordering and meaning dynamics of each dynamic. Repeat the click on Level 2, and each dynamic opens to Level 3 for further definition.

Opening up a Dynamic for More Definition

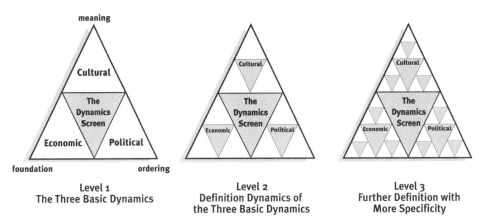

Level 1	Level 2	Level 3
The Three Basic Dynamics	Definition Dynamics of the Three Basic Dynamics	Further Definition with More Specificity

Figure 5

Continuing to click on each level reveals more specificity at each deeper level.

To go deeper in the dynamics in the model, examine the Further Definition – the Three Basic Dynamics in Figures 6a, 6b, and 6c. The what (foundation), how (ordering) and why (meaning) of each dynamic is pictured.

Further Definition – Three Basic Dynamics
Level 2

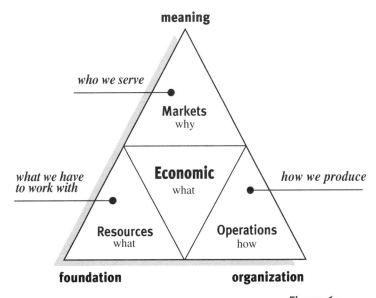

Figure 6a

The resources (what), operations (how) and markets (why) are what make up the Economic Dynamic (Figure 6a). Resources, the foundation (at the lower left of the graphic) are *what* we work with to provide goods and/or services. Resources include people, tables, computers, money, employable skills and so on. Markets, customers, products and services as well as sales strategy give meaning – the *why* – to the Economic Dynamic. The *how* of the Economic Dynamic – Operations – includes systems designs, quality measurements, specialization in the labor of leadership and employees. The tension between what is needed to sustain the enterprise (the resources – what) and customer needs (markets – why) drives operations (how) to achieve quality in products and services.

Further Definition – Three Basic Dynamics
Level 2

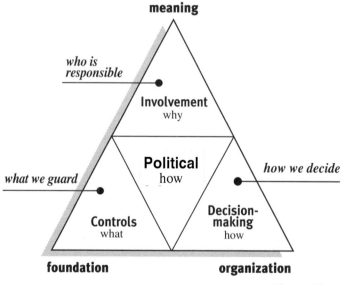

Figure 6b

In the Political Dynamic (Figure 6b) the foundation – the *what* – is administrative controls, such as fiscal guidelines, legal codes, monitoring structures. Controls and regulations are foundational to getting things organized. Decision-making is the ordering process – the *how* – and includes consensus process, leadership support, fair judgments, clear expectations and regular accountability. The *why* in the Political Dynamic is involvement, and includes information access, employee rights, quality work life, fair benefits and individual liberties. The tension between controls (what) and involvement of people (why) is what shapes the way decisions (how) are made.

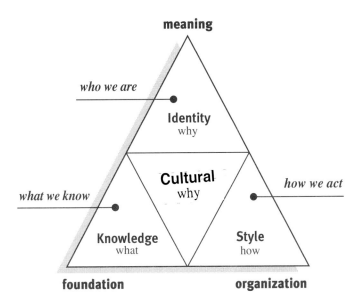

Further Definition – Three Basic Dynamics Level 2

Figure 6c

The foundation – the *what* – of the Cultural Dynamic (Figure 6c) is knowledge, including fundamental expertise, innovative methods, technical competence, shared values and social responsibility. Style, which includes individual roles, team spirit, continuous learning, team mix and flexible configurations – *how* – is the organizing dynamic. Meaning and direction – *why* – are in our identity: defined mission, space design, time patterns, unique language and compelling story. It is in the tension between knowledge (what) and an organization's identity (why) that the need to redefine style (how) is seen.

Reflect on the dynamics in your workplace.
- Identify the dynamics in your team/department
- Think about what happens when there are changes in the purpose/mission
- Clarify which dynamics are working together, which are working against each other

Reflective Learning

Thinkabouts in Dynamic Complexity

1. All the dynamics of an organization are interrelated. As a result, changes in one dynamic impact the others.
2. When the dynamics work together, change efforts work together and mixed messages are eliminated.
3. Identity is the key to balance. When you are clear about who you are and what your purpose is, there is more clarity about where to spend your time and energy in the other dynamics.
4. Apply the Dynamics Screen to a familiar organization. Figure 7 is an example of the dynamics in McDonald's. It describes some of the ways the dynamics are acted out in that organization.

Thinkabout

The examples in the Dynamics Screen in Figure 7 are some of the ways you see the dynamics being acted out in McDonald's. As the emphasis is shifting from quality, affordable meals to appeal to families with children's playgrounds and happy meals, energy and emphasis shift in all the dynamics. Dynamics are interrelated and shift with changes in customer demands.

Develop a New Field of Vision

The term "learning organization" has become increasingly popular as organizations and teams seek to discover how people continually learn from each other on the job. For any organization to become a learning organization requires developing new capacities and making fundamental shifts from linear thinking to systems thinking and from detail complexity to dynamic complexity thinking. The Dynamics Screen gives us a new way of seeing as we analyze why things are as they are.

As we grow into the full impact of the new economy, a greater balance between the economic (what we do), political (how we do it) and cultural (why

Application of Dynamics Screen to McDonald's

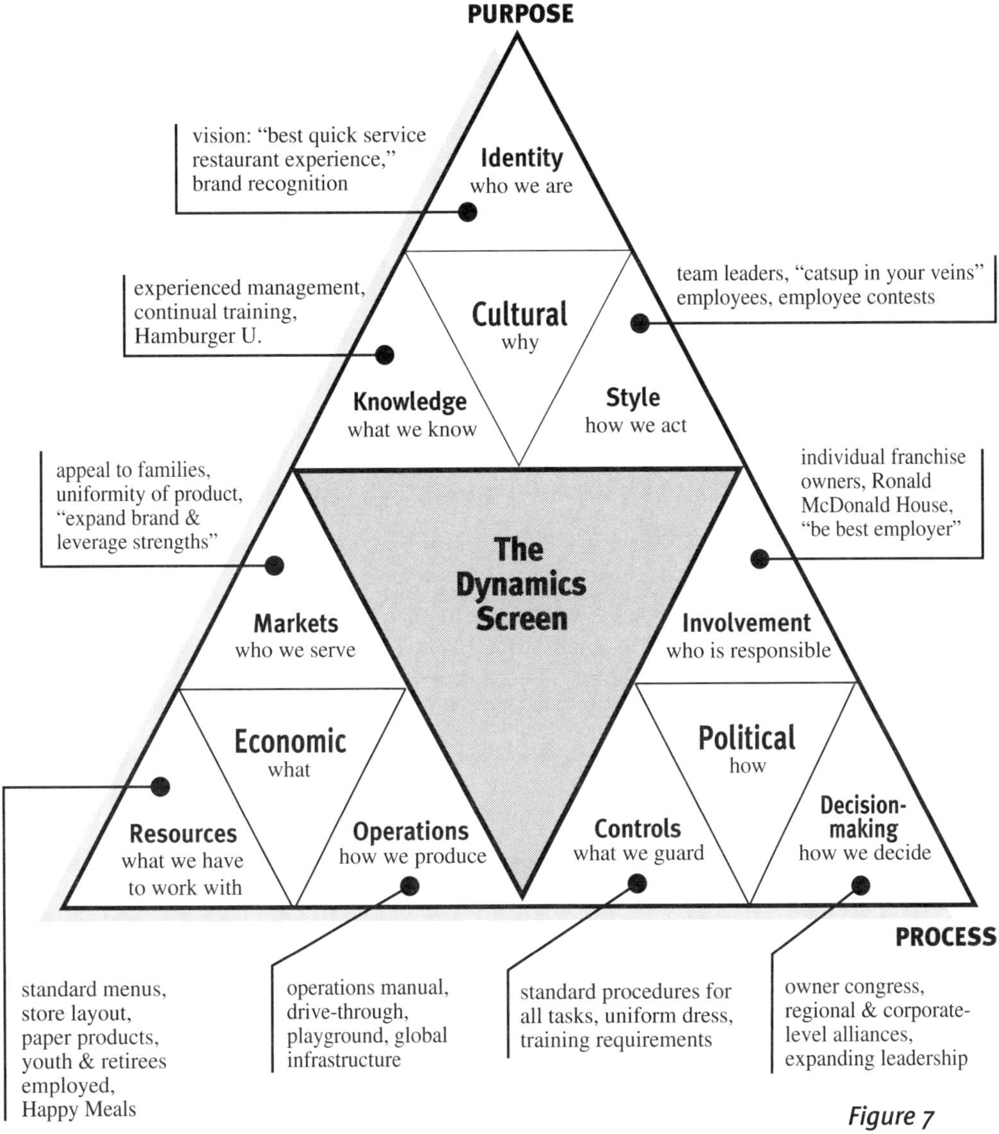

vision: "best quick service restaurant experience," brand recognition

experienced management, continual training, Hamburger U.

appeal to families, uniformity of product, "expand brand & leverage strengths"

PURPOSE

Identity
who we are

Cultural
why

team leaders, "catsup in your veins" employees, employee contests

Knowledge
what we know

Style
how we act

individual franchise owners, Ronald McDonald House, "be best employer"

The Dynamics Screen

Markets
who we serve

Involvement
who is responsible

Economic
what

Political
how

Resources
what we have
to work with

Operations
how we produce

Controls
what we guard

Decision-making
how we decide

PROCESS

standard menus, store layout, paper products, youth & retirees employed, Happy Meals

operations manual, drive-through, playground, global infrastructure

standard procedures for all tasks, uniform dress, training requirements

owner congress, regional & corporate-level alliances, expanding leadership

Figure 7

we do it) perspectives is required to build a complete bottom line. If we are to prosper, our cultural perspectives must be very strong. In the midst of so much change, they are the anchor. The stronger we believe in our purpose and values, the more we can change what we do and how we do it. Of the three perspectives, the cultural is generally given the least attention. Yet, it is what empowers people to take responsibility.

Understanding these dynamics has long been a part of human knowledge. In 350 BCE, Aristotle proposed that when a human being's basic drive of self-preservation, which is foundational (*economic*), is brought together with the drive for meaning (*cultural*), it results in the drive for order (*political*) or the social aspect of life.

Use the Dynamics Screen to filter customer or worker experience. When people are not engaged or providing the excellence demanded, apply organizational dynamics to operate strategically by reading what is really going on.

Figure 8 presents an example of applying the Dynamics Screen to a worker issue – how one manager thought about all the dynamics in order to be comprehensive as she faced a difficult situation.

By thinking through each of the dynamics in the formation of a new centralized unit, the manager ensured that all aspects of the situation were covered. Leaving out any dynamic could have caused prolonged turmoil for the department assistants. Because of the big-picture thinking of the manager for the new unit, work progressed smoothly as the team members addressed the issues in each of the dynamics.

As people experience more of a need to make sense of what is going on in their workplace, the Cultural Dynamics become more significant. Change is now the norm. Everything is up for grabs. What we counted on in the past is not here today. Help people overcome uncertainty by working to energize purpose, values and ownership. The object is to change the relationship from me-they to we. As one person put it, "It is the difference between hiring out as a mercenary and becoming a Marine."

Tips for balancing the dynamics include the following:
- When the Economic Dynamics are overemphasized, we are expending too much energy on short-term results, technical capabilities or pricing.
- When the Political Dynamics are overemphasized, we become bureaucratic, with too many layers of management control to get decisions made.
- When the Cultural Dynamics are overemphasized, we are probably discussion bound, endlessly asking "why" and never making a decision.

A Thinking Application of the Dynamics Screen

The Situation: No additional assistant positions could be funded despite an increasing workload. All departmental assistants would form a new centralized unit to serve departmental administrative needs. Assistants had previously worked in specific departments. The manager of the new unit used her understanding of how the organization works to get a big-picture perspective of what she needed to consider. This was her thinking:

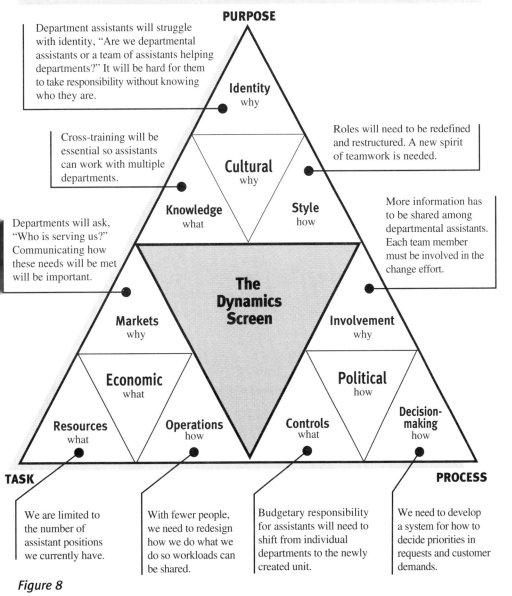

Figure 8

Thinkabouts for the Dynamics in Your Team/Organization

Thinkabout

Economic Dynamics

- What are the different kinds of resources needed?
- What are the internal and/or external client needs and services you provide?
- What operating systems, special abilities and measurements do you have?

Political Dynamics

- What policies, procedures, regulations and other controls exist?
- What do people need in order to feel like they are engaged in the task?
- What are some of the ways you make decisions?

Cultural Dynamics

- What values, methods and skills do you use in your work?
- How would other people describe who you are by looking at your work environment and listening to you talk?
- What best describes your roles, attitudes and behaviors?

Get Out of the *How* and Into the *Why*

For most of the past century most decisions – personal, professional and organizational – were made from an economic perspective. "Who are you?" usually meant "What job do you hold?" The organizing dynamics were under-emphasized and the cultural dynamics were virtually ignored. Much of the anger and frustration in our workplaces comes because people do not understand why we do what we do. We talk about what needs to be done and how it needs to be done, but we rarely talk about why it needs to be done. Remember this phrase? "Ours is not to reason why, ours is but to do or die." Maybe that sentiment motivated us in the past, but it doesn't today. If we are depending on the energies of people rather than machines, we had better focus on why. Rebalance the dynamics of your organization by emphasizing the *why* of the task. Emphasizing *why* we do *what* we do will energize people for the *how* (action).

Choices in the way organizations conduct their business are being challenged by today's marketplace demands. Figure 9 illustrates three marketplace demands, some of the challenges and choices as well as the key mindset to create.

Challenges in Today's Organizations

Dynamic Tension	Marketplace Demand	Choices	Key Mindset to Create
Economic Tension *(triangle diagram: tension, Markets, affect, Resources, E, Operations)*	**Do more with less**	Drive innovation or Experience being overwhelmed	Challenge the situation. *What do we need to start doing, stop doing, keep doing or do differently?*
Political Tension *(triangle diagram: tension, Involvement, affect, Controls, P, Decision-making)*	**Not either/or but both/and**	Create balance or Become highly bureaucratic or excessively participatory	Recognize the need for both bureaucratic structures and participation. *What is the role each can play?*
Cultural Tension *(triangle diagram: tension, Identity, affect, Knowledge, C, Style)*	**Do what we say; say what we do**	Be consistent or Create mixed messages and cross-purposes	Walk the talk. *Keep what is in sync. Change what is not.*

Figure 9

The team leader tells the group gathered around the table, "OK, now that we have this report back, I want you to form teams of three. I want each team to analyze the report from a communication viewpoint. Make sure your points are understandable. Are there any questions?" After a brief pause, a woman speaks up, "Why are we doing this?"

We need meaning and relevance for our actions. We need to connect what we are doing to a bigger picture. *Why* may even touch our emotions and spark ownership for the task.

People function better and deliver a more appropriate product if the context is established.

Why provides a rationale so people are motivated to innovate the "how."

We all have a "why" for what we do. When "why" isn't provided, we make it up. A "why" made up may not be appropriate for the given situation.

Think about your own workplace experiences.
- When have you experienced or been aware of a situation where the "why" was missing?
- What happened as a result?

Align Dynamics So They Work Together

"The main job of managers is to provide employees with a conceptual framework that helps them make sense of their own experience."
– Ikujiro Nonaka[10]

Aligning the dynamics to stamp out mixed messages is crucial for building internal commitment. A key thinking strategy is to recognize the interrelationship of the dynamics and to think through how each dynamic is being emphasized.

The bank teller aligning the dynamics in a needed change is one example. Changing a bank's customer service and the role of the tellers illustrates a thinking process for alignment.

1. Recognize the marketplace/customer forces that are driving the change.
   Customers want to walk into the bank and be greeted by tellers who know the bank's products and services and can handle customer questions. The goal is to create an organization of independent thinkers who take responsibility for meeting customer demands.

This wasn't new information to this bank. Cross-selling promotions and customer service training had made some difference. Nevertheless, when thinking through the nine dynamics (identity, markets, knowledge, style, involvement, controls, decision-making, resources and operations), the bank's branch managers realized they were sending mixed messages. As a result, they developed a more comprehensive plan for serving their customers.

2. Shape the emphasis in the Identity Dynamic to work with these forces.

The key is to align all the dynamics to help tellers see themselves as salespeople and decision-makers rather than just transaction processors.

3. Change the emphasis, as needed, in each of the other eight dynamics so that mixed messages are stamped out.

The branch managers recognize the need to change the emphasis of the other eight dynamics to support the message that tellers are also salespeople.

- *Markets Dynamic.* Help tellers recognize opportunities to cross-sell and handle complaints on the spot.
- *Knowledge Dynamic.* Provide sales training and rethink the current training. Model operating values to reflect the importance of the teller's role.
- *Style Dynamic.* Create a team spirit between tellers and personal bankers.
- *Involvement Dynamic.* Allow access to information about all bank services, so tellers can responsibly cross-sell.
- *Controls Dynamic.* Reconsider job descriptions. Examine policies. Make allowances for mistakes with an emphasis on learning from them.
- *Decision-Making Dynamic.* Communicate clear expectations about decision-making authority. Tellers need to know that their decisions will be supported (when the decision was obviously thought through) even if they result in errors.
- *Resources Dynamic.* Make sure all tellers have the technological capability to retrieve customer information on-line.
- *Operations Dynamic.* Change certain benchmarks. For example, referrals are as important as the number of transactions.

- From your experience in working with organizations, departments, teams, people – think about some of the classic mixed messages that are sent when dynamics are not aligned.

Reflective Learning

A manager and two supervisors of a surgery nursing team were requested by the nursing vice president to "speak with one voice" rather than continue to give conflicting messages on the unit.

A consultant met with each of them to hear individual views first. Each expressed a different idea of her role and the purpose of the unit. As a result, the first task was to clarify these differences and the benefit of working together.

In order to think together about what "speaking with one voice" could look like, each stated her expectations for the unit. Differences between their approaches and those of the larger unit became apparent as the exact words of each were recorded on the white board. They were now able to reflect on the expectation statements so that both common ideas and differences were recognized.

These commonalities and differences were put on hold while they wove a picture of where the unit had been and where it was going. A wall of Post-it™ notes was created to record past accomplishments, allowing them to see their own contributions as critical to the success of the unit. Each then posted six to eight anticipated happenings for the next three months.

Using the wall of accomplishments as the catalyst, each person took time to think and write down three stories – a funny story, a frustrating story and a meaningful story. Then, as they listened to each other tell their stories, a different perspective of their individual roles began to emerge. The funny stories noticeably picked up the energy in the room, the frustrating stories created a new empathy and the meaningful stories gave pause as they reflected on the importance of each one to the team.

The expanded context revealed how their roles complemented rather than competed with each other. The differences were located in the details, and the commonalities were part of the bigger picture. Relief and appreciation began to flow and a new sense of expectations for the unit began to emerge. They collaborated on creating a symbol for the unit of their combined leadership. First they worked individually on some elements for the symbol and then they combined the elements. After two to three redrawing exercises, one volunteered to put the result on paper to be hung in each of their offices.

Meeting several weeks later, they talked about how the symbol gave them a different way to relate to the rest of the unit. They experienced being a team "speaking with a common voice."

The Dynamics Screen helped the nurses reflect on identity, values and roles in a nonthreatening, often funny, way. Capturing that experience in a visual symbol for each of their offices gave them a new identity and became a daily reminder of their decision to "speak with one voice." Thus a more cooperative, unified tone and style emerged, reinforcing the unity of the unit. In using their energy to focus on identity, values and roles, these three nursing unit leaders leveraged their energy for maximum benefit to the unit.

Reflective Learning

- Take a few minutes to think about how the Dynamics Screen can help you operate strategically.

Understanding these dynamics and comprehending their interrelationships allows us to use our energy with the most leverage. As Peter Senge[11] discusses in *The Fifth Discipline,* "The real leverage in most management situations lies in understanding dynamic complexity, not detail complexity."

The Dynamic Screen is a tool for:
- understanding dynamic complexity
- locating points of leverage to effectively implement strategic action
- managing the context

Use Leverage to Mobilize Strategic Action

"When we give up myopic attention to details and stand far enough away to observe the movement of the total system, we develop a new appreciation for what is required to manage a complex system."
—Margaret Wheatley[12]

Focus on Nine Points of Leverage

After you have taken into account all the dynamics, how can your actions be more strategic, more focused? That is, how can you best allocate time, energy and resources?

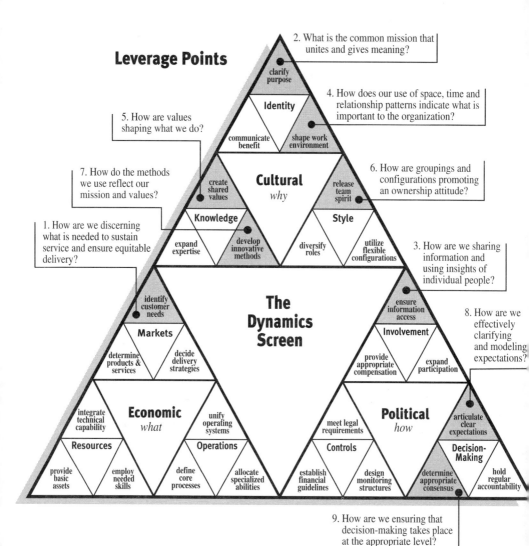

Leverage Points

2. What is the common mission that unites and gives meaning?

4. How does our use of space, time and relationship patterns indicate what is important to the organization?

5. How are values shaping what we do?

6. How are groupings and configurations promoting an ownership attitude?

7. How do the methods we use reflect our mission and values?

1. How are we discerning what is needed to sustain service and ensure equitable delivery?

3. How are we sharing information and using insights of individual people?

8. How are we effectively clarifying and modeling expectations?

9. How are we ensuring that decision-making takes place at the appropriate level?

clarify purpose

Identity

communicate benefit

shape work environment

create shared values

Cultural
why

release team spirit

Knowledge

Style

expand expertise

develop innovative methods

diversify roles

utilize flexible configurations

identify customer needs

The Dynamics Screen

ensure information access

Markets

Involvement

determine products & services

decide delivery strategies

provide appropriate compensation

expand participation

integrate technical capability

Economic
what

unify operating systems

meet legal requirements

Political
how

articulate clear expectations

Resources

Operations

Controls

Decision-Making

provide basic assets

employ needed skills

define core processes

allocate specialized abilities

establish financial guidelines

design monitoring structures

determine appropriate consensus

hold regular accountability

Figure 10

This is where leverage comes in. Using leverage means placing the most emphasis and energy to get maximum strategic advantage from your actions.

Experience with client organizations has shown us that certain dynamics in an organization provide more leverage than others. The nine points where leverage is most likely are shaded in Figure 10. Think through the questions as you reflect on your own team/organization. The leverage dynamics are numbered in order of importance.

The leverage point in the Economic Dynamic, identifying customer needs, drives everything in today's competitive marketplace. The five leverage points in the Cultural Dynamic are clarifying purpose, shaping the work environment, creating shared values, releasing team spirit and developing innovative methods. These dynamics are critical in creating an atmosphere of buy-in, synchronizing time and space with the purpose and ensuring the importance of people as a guiding principle for the organization. In today's workplace, team spirit is essential. Finally, the three leverage points in the Political Dynamic are ensuring information access, articulating clear expectations and determining appropriate consensus.

Since the greatest emphasis during the last three or four decades has been in the Economic Dynamics, it is not surprising that the greatest leverage today is in the Cultural Dynamics in order to rebalance thinking in an organization. Six of the nine leverage points are in the top third of their triangle – the *why* of that dynamic. Mobilizing energy around these dynamics will give the greatest impact.

You get the most results from your efforts (most effective leverage) when you:

1. Identify **customer needs** to understand the demands of today's marketplace.
2. Clarify **common purpose** to understand who you are and why you are involved in the organization. When the purpose changes, all the other dynamics must be realigned with the new purpose.
3. Make certain there is meaningful information access so people can be involved and engaged – **significant engagement**. The key is learning how to quickly extract meaning from data and information.
4. Reshape the **work environment** so the use of time, space and relationships supports the common purpose.
5. Create **shared values** that highlight what is important in the operating values. Operating values are changing:

from	to
"We have a job to do."	"Let's do what is needed."
"No one tells us anything."	"Who are we serving?"
"What are we doing?"	"What is our responsibility?"
"We can't try this."	"What would happen if?"

6. Release a **team spirit** that mobilizes energy and commitment with an entrepreneurial attitude.
7. Develop **innovative methods** to grow knowledge. Encourage and train people in leading facilitative conversations that solve problems, clarify issues, change work patterns and create new ideas.
8. Articulate **clear expectations** to empower people to act like owners and get things done. Model expectations consistently.
9. Provide support for **appropriate consensus** decision-making.

Finding the places of greatest leverage and prioritizing becomes the guide for moving strategically when managing change.

When change turns into a struggle, look at these leverage points to find what is needed. To assess where to get leverage in your organization, first determine what you think. Test out your thinking by talking with your coworkers, people in other departments and with customers to check out your perspective on what is needed.

(The Appendix includes the history of the Dynamics Screen, plus a copy of the Dynamics Screen for you to copy and use in your work. Also included are Economic, Political and Cultural Dynamic triangles with further definition at Level Four, plus a blank triangle for use as you think about the dynamics in your workplace.)

Align Everything with Serving the Customer

Maximize Leverage

The key in maximizing leverage is for everyone to know how he or she is serving the customer – the internal customers as well as the ultimate consumer. In an information economy, the manager removes the roadblocks and lets employees be in

How-to Action

control of the way they do their job. "Ah, but they can't handle all that responsibility," says the industrial-based manager. "They can handle it," says the information-based manager, "just look at what they do outside the workplace:
- hold a long-term view (e.g., mortgages, college funds)
- handle complex trade-offs (e.g., take a vacation vs. buy a car)
- self-manage situations (e.g., two working adults)
- develop budgets (e.g., better than Congress)
- deal with vendors and customers (e.g., every time they shop)
- manage projects (e.g., typical weekend work)."

When trying to maximize leverage, first observe what people care about, talk about and do. Then share information about customers, products, finances and competition to deepen awareness and build self-confidence and empowerment to sustain solutions over time in order to serve customers and represent the organization.

To find out where to focus your customer service efforts, assess, analyze and act on each of the leverage dynamics. The key is to assess where to put emphasis to make the most impact with your efforts. Below is an illustration of how to mobilize energy with leverage.

Strategically Mobilize Energy Using the Three "A" Steps
1. *Assess* what is going on (define the situation)
2. *Analyze* the information (as it pertains to the desired impact or change)
3. *Act* – decide which leverage points to address and in what order to realign the dynamics

Use these three steps as you work with each of the leverage dynamics.

• Customer Needs
1. Assess: What are the customers' needs? Are we responding to those needs?
2. Analyze: Is our position clear to the customer? If so, continue listening to customers in order to sustain effective responses. Does our brand stand out in the customer's mind as a product to meet his needs?
3. Act: If our position is not clear:
   - Develop our brand, image
   - Seed our reputation
   - Sharpen our expertise
   - Pay attention to what customers are saying

- **Common Purpose**
    1. Assess: What is the primary operating image or purpose as perceived by our employees and the public?
    2. Analyze: Is this well balanced with what is needed? If so, continue to clarify and communicate the purpose.
    3. Act: If not, change the image, redefine the purpose:
        - Clarify customer needs with more detailed assessment
        - Gather market data about what is needed – benchmark
        - Focus on the purpose in all efforts
        - Clarify expectations and accountability
- **Significant Engagement**
    1. Assess: What or how much do employees know about what is going on?
    2. Analyze: Do employees feel that they are "in the loop"? If so, continue the communication avenues that are working well and be alert for new avenues.
    3. Act: If not, mobilize employees for meaningful engagement:
        - Help employees get the information they need
        - Ask for individual insights
        - Delineate what and why and empower employees to decide how
        - Set priorities
- **Work Environment**
    1. Assess: What does the organization's use of time, space and working relationships say?
    2. Analyze: Does this align with the common purpose? If so, continue the effective use of time, space and relationships and stay alert for changes that better enable the purpose.
    3. Act: If not, realign:
        - Reprioritize time based on the strategically important issues rather than the urgent
        - Redesign space for logical work flow
        - Network people who need to work together
        - Provide opportunities for reflective dialogue
- **Shared Values**
    1. Assess: What do "we" consider important?
    2. Analyze: Do these operating values support the common purpose?

If so, continue to communicate these values in written and spoken communication.

3. Act: If not, reshape operating values:
   - Provide new data
   - Continually ask, "What is important?"
   - Challenge assumptions that support the values
   - Put people in situations where they can experience different operating values

- **Team Spirit**
  1. Assess: What are the formal and informal ways people interrelate?
  2. Analyze: Do we have the flexibility, respect and trust we need? If so, continue to encourage these ways of interrelating.
  3. Act: If not, encourage new ways of interrelating:
     - Find common tasks that require working across departments
     - Put people in cross-relationships
     - Use flexible assignments
     - Provide supportive structures

- **Innovative Methods**
  1. Assess: What are the processes and methods we use?
  2. Analyze: Are they helping us do what needs to be done the best way possible? If so, continue to incorporate these processes and methods into all new and continuing projects.
  3. Act: If not, create new innovative processes for accomplishing tasks, meeting goals/objectives:
     - Develop pilot projects using experimental procedures
     - Use think tanks to brainstorm
     - Apply process improvement analysis techniques
     - Change the way you conduct meetings

- **Clear Expectations**
  1. Assess: What are employees' expectations?
  2. Analyze: Are expectations aligned with the common purpose? If so, continue to be clear about expectations in all communication avenues.
  3. Act: If not, work to make things more clear:
     - Model what is expected of employees
     - Create accountability structures
     - Support people at critical times with clear expectations

- **Appropriate Consensus**
    1. Assess: What are the modes of decision-making?
    2. Analyze: Do decision-making modes match the level of engagement required by the situation? If so, continue these levels of engagement in decision-making.
    3. Act: If not, clarify appropriate decision-making modes/models:
        - Demonstrate what consensus is and is not; consensus is about moving together (See Ignite Action, page 154).
        - Clarify the appropriate decision-making mode for the current situation (some decisions need to come down from above, some decisions just require input while yet others need to involve more people)
        - Involve the people impacted by the decision in the decision-making (perhaps not everyone in every meeting, but a representative, rotating cross-section); devise a way to keep people updated
        - Keep a balance between too little and too much involvement

To effectively manage change using the leverage points, step back and think about your assessment and analysis of the leverage points. There is no one right answer. The *what* and *why* in a given situation shape *how* something is done. For instance, when the purpose becomes clear (not what is talked about), decisions are made about how to reflect the purpose in the working environment. The values we hold – what we consider important – shape the kinds of methods used with a particular group of people. Working with leverage dynamics ensures strategic action. Working with a leverage dynamic that impacts several others maximizes strategic impact. When a focus on *shared values* includes a desire to meet customers' needs, people pull together with a new sense of *common purpose* and experience a need to create *innovative methods* to meet these needs.

When the board and staff of a facility for the homeless examined their vision and values, they decided two key values were (a) the dignity of each person and (b) support systems to help individuals improve their situations. This led to a new sense of common purpose to deepen current programs and explore new service responses. They created innovative methods to redesign the two-week transitional living period into a healing period and new community-based permanent housing.

Reflective Learning

Shifts in the workplace today are being driven by marketplace forces of:

- expanding customer choice
- global competition
- constant change

Consumers are driving these forces. Consequently, it is important to know as much about the customer and the competition as possible.

Involve others in completing the following assessment exercise. Use it several times. It will become a measure of progress in how customer satisfaction and dissatisfaction is perceived.

1. Who are our customers? (internal and external)
2. What are our customers' expectations? What delights them?
3. What products/services do we provide to our customers?
4. What is your role in providing products/services?
5. Who is our competition?
6. What does our competition do well?
7. What is our strength? What do we do well?
8. What will it take to stay ahead of the competition?
9. What role do we each need to play in this?

> **"Problems and proposed solutions are often like icebergs: What is visible at first glance often turns out to be only a small portion."**
> **– Gerald Nadler[13]**

Do What Matters

Clarity of purpose helps us understand who we are and why we are involved in an organization. As mentioned, when the purpose shifts, all the other dynamics are called into question.

A hospital dietary team was having trouble delivering hot meal trays to remote sites. After struggling for several months to keep the food warm, the question of their purpose (who they are and what they do) was raised. The team stated they were responsible for the "dine-in food service." Immediately the problem became clear. "We are trying to use a dine-in system to do carry-out food. Our purpose is both dine-in and carry-out." Once they recognized this change of purpose, they were able to realign what they were doing and were subsequently able to do their job more effectively.

Think about this dietary team as they realized their purpose was to be both "dine-in" and "carry-out." At the moment of that insight, the big picture changed. Their expertise needed to grow, roles had to change, new operating systems were required, and so on. The new purpose demanded a review of every existing structure and relationship to create the match between what they thought they were doing and what needed to be done.

Another team in an established organization felt increased pressure to reduce costs and increase quality of service. In spite of meetings and brainstorming sessions, all ideas seemed to fall flat. As a result, team members felt powerless and overwhelmed.

The team finally used the Dynamic Screen to help them articulate what they wanted (their vision) and to assess the challenges to getting there. The Dynamics Screen guided their thinking by defining ways to increase quality of service while reducing costs.

Using the screen helped them structure their conversations. Specifically, (a) they each expressed concerns and ideas, and (b) they reviewed the team's identity and made sure to align goals, tasks and projects with that identity. First they asked questions about their vision (what they wanted) in each of the dynamics. After there was clarity about their vision, they asked questions about the challenges they faced in each dynamic. This allowed more comprehensive choices to be made.

- Think about an area where you need to do what matters. This might include a project or initiative you are implementing, working with your team, the department you are in, and so on. If working on a leverage dynamic that impacts several others maximizes strategic impact, where do you need to focus your energy and why?

Reflective Learning

Manage the Context

**"The significant problems we face
cannot be solved at the same level we were
at when we created them."
—Albert Einstein**

Change is coming at Stuart faster than he can assimilate it. A unit manager, his team is pushing his frustration level higher and higher. Some people are constantly tardy, others are repeatedly late for work. Stuart thinks that tighter policy controls are the only answer.

At lunch one day, Stuart sees Denzel sitting at a table by himself. Remembering that Denzel once said, "I'm going to guide change, not fight it," Stuart wants to know how that idea is working for him and goes over to sit down across from him. "Help," Stuart starts. Denzel raises his eyebrows. "What's wrong?" "I've lost control," Stuart explains, picking up his fork. "I don't know how to handle my team."

Denzel nods sympathetically. "I felt that way before I went to that conference last month. I was about to tear out my hair" – Denzel pats his bald head. "That conference let me look at my team in a new way." Denzel then proceeds to explain the facilitative outlook he gained from the training:

- *Assume that the people on your team are creative, thinking people.*
- *Look for their strengths and challenges.*
- *Create and communicate a vision.*
- *Discover the organization's core values.*
- *Forge a new sense of interdependence.*
- *Ask questions and listen for insights in every situation to guide and help people make sense of what is going on.*

Denzel wraps up his newly learned insights as follows, "If we are going to find the leverage in every situation, we have to give up the overseer's job. This means managing the context people work in differently. We need to serve the people we used to boss. We have to support what they need so they can be more responsive to customers. We use our expertise to facilitate their work. We use our time to eliminate the barriers and bottlenecks that affect the job to be done."

Here are some of the techniques Denzel is using to leverage his team and their knowledge. To ensure economic survival he encourages the team to pay attention to the market dynamics by incorporating a vibrant customer consciousness. In every task he asks:

"What are we doing to find out our customers' (internal and external) expectations?"

"What are we doing to meet these expectations?"

To strengthen the Cultural Dynamics of the team and the overall organization, he is emphasizing identity, style and knowledge by asking questions and listening for insights in every situation to guide and help people make sense of what is going on:

"What is the compelling story of who we are and what we do?"

"How are we communicating the benefits of being who we are?"

"What elements in our working space and our relationships give us a clear sense of what we are about?"

"What does each of us think is important that reflects the shared values we hold?"

"How does the way we work together build a spirit of ownership?"

"What innovative methods are you using that are helpful and why?"

Focus on the Political Dynamic will build new levels of involvement and decision-making. Denzel is asking questions and listening for (i.e., paying attention to) what is going on in order to honor and defend people's work:

"How are we making sure that people have the information they need to be most effective?"

"How are we clarifying expectations?"

"What decisions are pushing power to the frontline and how are we doing that?"

In order to have a "doing the work responsibly" team, he thinks about the leverage points in every situation. He remembers to strategically mobilize energy using the three "A" steps (see pages 47-50).

Do you know your way around so that team members are connecting with each other, the task and the purpose?

If connections are still missing, you will see and hear:
- hall meetings that are separate and exclusive
- people staying in their cubby holes
- continued tardiness and absences

- defensive comments
- nonproductive silences
- finger-pointing and blame

If connections are being made, you will see and hear:

- participation and engagement
- people being quicker to respond
- conversations carrying the task forward
- sharing of information
- accepting responsibility
- contribution from many group members, not just from one

The complexity of today's changes can defeat even what we consider our best solutions. "Everything seems to be connected to everything else" is a common way people refer to this complexity. The challenge? We have to upgrade our problem-solving thinking.

Complex change requires that we keep both the big picture and the details in mind when we think through problems, issues, strategies and tasks.

Summary

Understand your organization as a system of dynamic relationships and then take its pulse using these dynamics. Today's marketplace with extensive customer choice, vast competition and constant change is shifting the way we respond to these dynamics, calling for comprehensive systemic thinking.

Learn how to hold the relationship between the detailed task and the big picture. When thinking is done with consistency and intent using the system's dynamics, you are able to choose the action that is critical to the organization and create the necessary commitment to get things done.

As you come to understand the dynamic complexity in your team and organization, you will discover where to focus your energy. This in turn brings new intentionality and strategy to your efforts. Concentrate on the dynamics that give the most leverage and lead to action. Learn how to strategically seed thinking, find entry points, challenge comfort zones and energize momentum.

Orchestrate Interactions

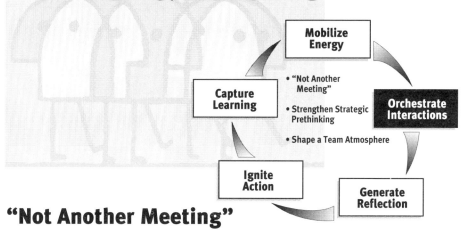

Mobilize Energy

- "Not Another Meeting"
- Strengthen Strategic Prethinking
- Shape a Team Atmosphere

Capture Learning

Orchestrate Interactions

Ignite Action

Generate Reflection

"Not Another Meeting"

Meetings, meetings, meetings! No one wants one more meeting. Have you ever:

- sat through part of a meeting wondering, "What are we trying to accomplish here?"
- participated in a discussion that changed subjects in the middle?
- ended up frustrated by an interaction that wandered aimlessly from topic to topic?
- experienced heading down one path then later realizing that things had somehow shifted to a new direction?

We have all sat through endless meetings. Yet even with so many meetings, we can still experience inadequate information, false assumptions and decisions made and not shared. We are often blindsided when a meeting has not been thought through in advance.

Meeting Nightmares

Battle of Opinions

Sam, the lead person, starts the meeting. "I hope each of you has taken the opportunity to review the proposal on flex time since this is an issue near and dear to us all. Time is of the essence, so let's get right down to it."

A familiar scenario is now unleashed. A battle of opinions begins – Sue says she sees the need for further research into the impact of flex time on the customer. Roberto urges the group to get more input from employees. Shawn doesn't want to offer flex time to her staff.

After forty minutes of diverse opinions, Sam finally stands up, puts his palms flat on the table and says, "It is obvious that we have a variety of opinions. I was hoping that we could reach consensus today but that doesn't seem possible. Let's put this aside for now so we have more time to think on this."

Sam leaves the meeting frustrated and unsure about how to end the battle of opinions. He knows the next meeting will result in the same process all over again with the same result: inaction.

Off-Track Discussions

Contractor accountability is the top item on the agenda as the manager, Sara, begins the meeting. She intends to focus on particular problems experienced lately with the contractors, but the discussion wanders off and soon they are talking about how the teams are operating. Suddenly they are immersed in team politics, trying to describe the whole elephant instead of solving the small problem Sara first raised.

This meeting is going nowhere except off track with lengthy discussion. Sara decides to assign some homework in hopes the next meeting can accomplish something. "What we need is some specific information on what the contractors actually should be doing. Will you each bring to the next meeting a list of particular needs in your area that you want to contract out."

Information Dump

The ABC Team was formed three months ago, but it is becoming clear that the regularly scheduled weekly meetings have gotten into a rut. Rather than purposeful meetings, nothing is planned. A "talking at" mode of information dump has turned the meetings into a routine that isn't engaging anyone.

Marie decides to speak up, "Since weekly meetings are expected of us, let's have a different format each time. We could brainstorm an issue; do problem solving; have a decision-making meeting; even an information meeting. We could have a storytelling meeting about our accomplishments. That would work if we take time to reflect on what we've learned." Relieved that some-

body has new ideas, ABC team members agree to try this idea. They create a flexible schedule and each person chooses which type of meeting he or she wants to lead.

Start Where People Are

Five department teams are required to attend a two-day training class on team building. The trainers are caught up in their "really good plan" and don't notice until mid-day that one team is struggling – team members are sitting still but quietly sabotaging the process with their comments. By the end of the day the facilitators realize they can't get the team engaged. Upon reflection they realize that they have forgotten the cardinal rule of "start where people are." The non-engaged team has spent the morning using a lot of energy blaming each other and recriminating about real and perceived hurts.

The facilitators try a different approach the second day. One facilitator works with the disengaged team. She focuses questions on the team's work and relationships and listens carefully as the team shares their diverse perspectives. As each team member is heard and affirmed, the atmosphere shifts from sniping conversations to sharing information. Team members discover they are able to work together in new ways.

Good meetings, helpful conversations and other effective interactions don't just happen. When the manager defines what needs to be done and why, there has been a lot of input from employees. Together the manager and team discover ways to best implement the goals.

Watch for the red flags that tell you there is no focus in a meeting:
- Wandering comments – the "why?" question asked over and over
- Unconnected thinking – a key image is missing
- No listening to each other – people are pushing for just their own agenda

Don't be out of date and out of touch in the interactions that take place daily. The starting point for not getting caught off guard is thorough preparation. Be strategic in thinking ahead about what needs to happen. Orchestrate interactions on behalf of the people involved and the task at hand with strategic prethinking to build on where people are in their thinking and design methods that enable people to think together.

Strengthen Strategic Prethinking

**"Either you spend energy creating what you want,
or you spend energy coping with what you have."
– Anonymous**

Change Your Reference Point

When you decide you need new ways of asking questions and relating to people so they can assume more responsibility, you increase the need to plan how the meeting will go, including a flow of diverse ideas, a dialogue to increase understanding and a method for arriving at the intended outcome.

Most meetings don't work because no one is being facilitative and making them work. Think in advance about what needs to happen to maximize the use of time. Behind every effective interaction is strategic prethinking and intentional scripting. Depending on the complexity of the meeting, this process can take from a few minutes to several hours and may need lots of interfacing with those involved. We will take a look at the components of the process for prethinking below.

Before orchestrating meetings or other interactions, decide how best you can be facilitative and ease the process for the group. In the following story (author unknown) a carpenter uses a symbol to remind him of his choice to ease things for his family.

I hired a carpenter to help me restore an old farmhouse. A flat tire made him lose an hour of work, his electric saw quit, and when he was ready to quit for the day his ancient pickup truck refused to start. It was a rough first day on the job.

While I drove him home, the carpenter sat in stony silence. When we got there, he invited me in to meet his family. As we walked toward the front door, he paused briefly at a small tree, touching the tips of the branches with both hands.

When he opened the door, he underwent an amazing transformation. His lined face was all smiles as he hugged his two small children and gave his wife a kiss.

As he walked me back out to my car, we passed the tree again and my curiosity got the better of me. I asked him about what I had seen him do earlier.

"Oh, that's my trouble tree," he replied. "I know I can't help having troubles on the job, but one thing's for sure, troubles don't belong in the house with my wife and the children. So I just hang them up on the tree every night when I come home. Then in the morning I pick them up again."

"Funny thing is," he smiled, "when I come out in the morning to pick 'em up, there aren't nearly as many as I remember hanging up the night before."

When you decide to be facilitative, hang your personal troubles on the doorknob before you enter a room to work with others.

Thinkabouts

Thinkabout

- Find out where people are … and begin the journey with them from there.
- Facilitate shared ownership for the interaction and its outcome.
- When in doubt, ask the group what is needed.

Prepare the Orchestration

Facilitative Approach

The goal of strategic prethinking is to orchestrate an effective gathering that energizes participants and encourages them to contribute their best. It can turn the "dull" into an invigorating happening. Orchestration focuses our expectations for the group and shapes the environment, style and mode to reinforce those expectations.

An important aspect of strategic prethinking is to intentionally shift the focus from the leader's expectations and objectives to the group's expectations and objectives. The Prethinking Guidelines in Figure 1 (page 62) suggest actions that can help you shift your focus from an "I" focus to a "we" facilitative strategic approach.

Orchestrating interactions can be strategic and facilitative or it can be manipulative and directive. Be aware of your own intentions; people will be able to tell the difference. Involve others in the facilitative and strategic prethinking.

Prethinking Guidelines

Shift		What to do
From **I**	**To** **WE** *Facilitative Strategic Approach*	**Action**
How can I achieve the outcome?	Ask, "How can WE achieve the outcome?"	Talk with enough people until you see how to achieve the outcome. (Gather data)
I build the agenda and we are ready to go.	Describe a way/scenario for others to see.	Share and check out your picture and scenario with others.
I present information, ask if everyone understands and then move on.	Give people the opportunity to make the information their own. Ask the group what is possible.	Get out hopes and dreams, name the roadblocks, focus the reflections, and get things on the table.
I assign the tasks to the large group or send a small group off to work on specific aspects.	Think about how to configure people most effectively.	Strategically chunk the information and reflect after each chunk.
I will plan some fun activity.	Make the task fun.	Use the dynamics of small group/large group to enhance participation, generate ideas and move more quickly.
I will use whatever space is available and use it "as is."	If necessary, rearrange the space guided by the scenario.	Get information on the space in advance. Arrive early enough so you can reconfigure as needed.
I will list the things we have to do and the amount of time we have.	Remember that people will make time for what they see as important.	Make a case for what it will take to do it together – and then let the group decide priorities and action plan.

Figure 1

Strategic Assessment

Every interaction has an outcome. Sometimes the outcome is assigned, as when the boss says, "Here is the result we need from the meeting next week." At other times you decide the outcome, as when, "The next meeting with my team needs to result in a strong commitment to finish the budget process." In either case the interaction requires strategic prethinking to ensure the outcome is achieved. That requires two major steps: (a) review the relevant data to assess how realistic the outcome is and (b) project how the outcome will be accomplished.

Step 1. Is the Desired Outcome Realistic and Relevant?

- *Realistic:*
    - What is the history of the outcome? Is this the right time to take this on?
    - What authority does this outcome require to be successful? Do you have the necessary authority?
    - Who are the critical people who need to be involved (and are they involved)?
    - What is the timeframe for achieving this?
    - What kind of commitment is needed? Can you get it?
- *Relevant:*
    - What is going on now as it relates to the desired outcome?
    - What support is there for this outcome?
    - Where is this outcome in the organization's priority list?
    - What is the connection between the desired outcome and the critical activity of the organization?

If the outcome is realistic, it is time to move to the second step. If it isn't, ask yourself and others what would make it realistic and act accordingly, or forget the whole idea.

Step 2. How Can We Accomplish This Outcome?

Once you determine that the outcome is indeed realistic, it is time to put the pieces together to guarantee success.

- What are the biggest challenges to achieving the outcome?
    - What has your assessment told you about available support, personnel needs, technical needs?
    - What are the biggest blocks (mindset, values, beliefs)?
    - What advantages do you have to overcome these blocks?

- Where is this outcome in the organization's priority list?
    - Is this an informed assumption? (check your assumptions with others)
    - Is the timing right to attempt this outcome?
    - Do you need to spend more time convincing influential people of the importance of the project?
    - Are other initiatives going on that might overshadow this effort?
- What authority will help the outcome be successful?
    - Be careful not to miscalculate here; check your estimate with others.
    - Did you describe the outcome in enough detail so decision-makers realize the potential impact on time, money and relationships? How do you know?
    - What support of the decision-makers do you have? Are resources, people and time allocated?
    - Are decision-makers talking with their peers about the outcome? What do they say?
- Which critical people need to be involved?
    - Make a list of people and why they are important to the outcome. Share this list with at least three others to get their input. If there are questions, get more input.
    - Make sure you have thought of all pertinent areas in projecting what it will take to meet the outcome.
    - Guard against making the outcome too big. Be mindful of what can be done in the given amount of time. You might need several meetings to accomplish what you hope to achieve.
- Reflect on upcoming situations to enhance your preparation.
    - Gather information about the situation. Determine any external factors that may influence the situation (celebrations, tragedies, stock market, rain, tax day, etc.).
    - What internal factors may influence the situation (who has previous experiences with the topic, the computers are down, a new person is coming on board, etc.)?

Design an Intentional Script

Decide the Intent

Having assessed how realistic the outcome is and projected how the outcome will be accomplished, prepare so people can think and take action together.

First, decide your intent for the meeting. That is your point of reference and helps you keep on track. Think about two sets of criteria:

1. What do people need to KNOW in order to accomplish the desired outcome?

Ask yourself and others questions like:

"What information is needed in advance and during the meeting/interaction?"

"What does this group need to think through together to reach the desired outcome?"

"What knowledge or insights need to be shared or uncovered?"

"What do people already know that needs to be drawn out?"

2. What do people need to EXPERIENCE in order to accomplish the desired outcome?

Ask yourself and others questions like:

"What is the shared emotion or experience we want people to have?"

"How will people relate to each other differently as a result of this?"

"How do we hope this alters people's thinking about this topic?"

If this is a large meeting or event, ask some of the participants what they expect to know and experience. Guard against making your intent too broad and tailor your intent to the people involved.

Thinkabouts ... Examples of Possible Intents

Thinkabout

To achieve the outcome, people need to KNOW:

- A common set of data and information
- Steps already taken
- Why they are being asked to participate
- Why a decision was made in the organization and needs to be discussed
- What has/has not worked before

To achieve the outcome, people need to EXPERIENCE:
- Possibility and vision
- A spirit of teamwork
- Being heard and understood
- A sense that this meeting is important
- That their participation makes a difference
- A sense of excitement

Think through the group dynamics:
- Will people know each other or need time to "warm up"?
- What levels of reporting relationships will be represented in the room?
- How many organizational levels will be represented in the room?
- Is this a risky topic for people?

Reflective Learning

Create the Context

As a manager, Michael has been thinking about the beginning of a new project for several days. When the group has its first meeting to discuss the project, Michael wonders why the team isn't as excited about the project as he is. Then he realizes that the others haven't been able to think about it in advance. They need a way (a context) to catch up and catch the excitement.

The "context" is what you say at the beginning of any interaction to help people focus their attention.

A context sets the stage and the tone to provide the starting place and direction for people's thinking.

Without a context, data wander randomly in people's brains, causing a slow start and sometimes blocking momentum. The context reflects the outcome and intent you already have in your mind. In addition to making it clear at the outset, be prepared to restate the context in the middle as needed to refocus the interaction.

The context helps everyone start together and stay together. Examples of the roles context plays include:

- To answer the question "why"
- To set the stage
- To broaden perspectives
- To recap the situation
- To share background information
- To "reframe" the topic or issue
- To encourage new action
- To relate this meeting to other activities if needed.

If you are sitting through a meeting wondering, "What are we trying to accomplish here?" it probably means that the context is missing.

Craft a context to trigger thinking. Include pertinent background information to help people share the same view. For example:

"We are being called on to take on roles outside of traditional job descriptions. As you know, our entire organization is rethinking the way it operates. It may help if we talked about these changes. We can examine the impact these changes have had and will continue to have on our roles. Are you willing to participate?"

Set the context at the beginning of any interaction to help people understand why they need to think together.

An effective context:

1. Describes the situation
2. Clarifies the outcome
3. States why this subject is important
4. Suggests a way to proceed
5. Asks for consensus to move together

An example interaction with outcome, intent and context is described below.
The *overall outcome* is to make the transition to a new computer system as seamless as possible for both the customer and the team.
The *outcome* for the next meeting is to identify and discuss the key changes and to minimize their impact.

The next meeting's *intent*:
- What the team *needs* to know is that change is affecting everyone. Also, they need to know the specific computer changes identified so far.
- What they *need to experience* is that we are all in this together, we are learning together and we can handle this.

An effective context for this interaction is illustrated in Figure 2.

Setting the Context

Elements	Example
1. Describe the situation.	"As you are all aware, the new computer system is all the buzz. Certainly, it is not new for any of us to experience change. In fact, our entire organization has been rethinking the way it operates now that the new computer system is on its way."
2. Clarify the outcome.	"I thought it would be helpful if we talked through the changes we are aware of, so we can examine the impact they may have and will continue to have on what we do."
3. State why it is important.	"By looking at this together, I hope we can learn from each other how to make this transition as seamless as possible."
4. Suggest a way to proceed.	"I thought we could brainstorm the changes and then list the impact of each. Then we can look for ways to make these changes less traumatic for our customers and for us."
5. Ask for consensus to move together	"Are there any questions about what we are doing? Can you make the commitment of time and energy to think about this."

Figure 2

Often the context needs to be reviewed and reset during an interaction. Again verbalize the five components.

1. Describe the current situation: "We have about twenty minutes left in our one hour meeting."

2. Clarify the outcome: "As you recall, we originally agreed to meet to review both the financial results and customer service results."

3. State why it is important: "Since both sets of numbers will inform this decision and we have spent significant time reviewing the financial results …"

4. Suggest a way to proceed: "Perhaps we should turn our attention now to the customer service results."

5. Ask for consensus to move together: "Are we ready to do this?"

Setting a clear context is like putting a fence around a playground. One study of the playing habits of kindergartners discovered that when there is no fence, children generally played in the center of the playground. With a fence around the playground the children used all the space for their play. Similarly, when a context sets the parameters around a subject, thinking can range across the whole spectrum of possibility. When no parameters are set, people impose their own limits and are much less creative in their thinking.

Thinkabouts for Setting the Context

Thinkabout

- The five elements of setting the context can be reordered as necessary to fit a given situation and the people involved.
- Not all five parts of a context must be statements. Two good elements for asking questions are clarifying the outcome ("From where you stand, how would you talk about the outcome we are trying to achieve?") and describing why it is important, ("From your perspective, why is this important?").
- Sometimes setting the context is brief and to-the-point. Other situations demand a more in-depth context. For example, contexts that work to broaden perspectives or reframe the issue tend to be more in-depth. The context helps us start to think together. Be aware that more words are not always the answer.
- When you ask for consensus to move together, clearly ask for consensus for the part of the context that is up for decision. Most often people find themselves asking for agreement regarding how to proceed, "Does this make sense as the first step? Are you willing to proceed as suggested?"

Figure 3 (page 70) illustrates the relationship between outcome, intent and context.

Outcome – Intent – Context

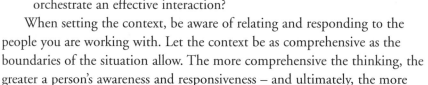

Figure 3

- Think about a meeting or interaction you have participated in where there was a clear context. What happened?
- When there was no clear context, what happened?
- How do a clear outcome, intent and context help orchestrate an effective interaction?

Reflective Learning

When setting the context, be aware of relating and responding to the people you are working with. Let the context be as comprehensive as the boundaries of the situation allow. The more comprehensive the thinking, the greater a person's awareness and responsiveness – and ultimately, the more responsibility will be taken for the task.

Shape a Team Atmosphere

"Vitality is proportional to intentionality."
– Paul Tillich[1]

Spark T-E-A-M-S

An atmosphere/environment that is supportive of people builds anticipation. It informs people that something, or nothing, is going to happen. This is as true in an interaction involving two people as it is for group interactions.

The meeting environment does as much or more to promote positive participation and productivity as other factors.

To create a productive meeting environment, preparation is key.

All five elements of T-E-A-M-S are needed to create a supportive environment for a meeting:

- Timeframe
- Eventfulness
- Accountability
- Methods
- Space

Working with all the factors to gain an edge within each enables us to be more intentional and shape a more productive, engaging environment.

Timeframe

How-to Action

Time is probably the most important resource for many people. To honor people's time, we let people know the timeframe for starting and ending. We set an agenda – and we stick to it.

To gain an edge, think about the strategic use of time more intentionally.

- Use momentum and timing as keys to people's sense of accomplishment. Decide when a pause for reflection will underscore what has been done and how.

- Strategically chunk time so tasks and reflections are focused.
- Plan breaks and humor to maximize participation and learning. Research indicates people remember the most just before and just after a break.
- Reflect at appropriate intervals so people hear from each other.
- Be aware of appropriate pacing (i.e., when things need to move quickly and when the group needs to spend more time).
- Carefully think through the opening and closing of a meeting, which serve as "book ends" for the time together.
- Assess the time needed for various components of the interaction:
    - information sharing
    - presenting and processing of information, models, reports, etc.
    - reflection time to enable understanding and ownership.

Eventfulness

The eventfulness in a meeting takes it out of the humdrum and makes it stand out. Participants experience the time together as important, eventful and momentous. In our work with organizations, we often plan eventfulness with stretch breaks, icebreakers, music, food and storytelling. We celebrate or dramatize important happenings.

To gain an edge, build in ways to vary the mood and rhythm depending on the intended effect. If the tone has been like a waltz, change the pattern to a jitterbug and vice versa.

Sometimes people need to move around. Listen to what people tell you and notice their body language. Be prepared to pick up the pace when you read the signals. Different rhythms can enliven participants at a particular time of day or can promote a particular kind of reflection. Sometimes the team needs structured ways to allow for more thinking and processing. Change your methods so people experience their participation as meaningful and exciting.

> *The planning and reporting sessions for the construction of a Medical Mall are complex and confusing. Verbal reports from the various departments seem unrelated to each other. Each department of the Medical Mall is going in its own direction. How can anyone keep track of the multiplicity of issues and successes as the opening of the Medical Mall nears? Progress report meetings have been long and laborious. Having struggled with this for a while, one manager suggests a different kind of weekly reporting session with a way to*

visually track what is happening. This suggestion leads to the creation of the "critical path" plan, which quickly becomes a swirl of eventfulness.

A huge time chart posted on the gym wall lists the twenty-five teams down the left side. Across the top are listed the eighteen weeks remaining before the Grand Opening. Excitement builds as each team posts events and accomplishments when they enter the gym for the weekly meeting. As people read the wall, the itemized events shift from being individual department items to the hospital's accomplishments. As many people as possible (given their work schedules) reflect weekly as the itemized lists grow. Questions that encourage reflection include:

- *What struck you as you read the wall?*
- *What surprised you? What was something you didn't know or remember?*
- *What were you the proudest of in your own or others' involvement?*
- *Where did you get worried about making it all come together?*
- *Where do you see turning points in the process?*
- *What most clearly signals the future of the hospital?*
- *What are critical decisions that have to be made between now and the opening?*

The gym wall becomes a center of attention as people congregate at various times of the day to watch the progress of the Mall plan. A new climate of trust and responsibility grows out of this process of eventfulness, sharing and accountability.

Accountability

**"People choose accountability, they aren't held accountable.
The price of accountability is to live with anxiety."
– Peter Block[2]**

When meetings are held, do you build in an understanding of who is responsible for what? Plan the interaction so there is a balance between expectations and accountability. When expectations are clear, it becomes apparent who is to account for actions and non-actions. Start by holding yourself accountable. Next, remind others they are accountable.

The Performance Review Team in a small investment firm considers their strategic plan quite good. Strategic plans have a habit of getting lost on a shelf so they know that having a good plan isn't enough. As a result, they create an action plan whereby each subteam is assigned specific tasks (e.g., compile a profile of customers; revise a performance document; rename and reorganize a project).

At the first meeting after developing the action plan, the action plan is the agenda. Assignments are checked and discussed. Team members remember when they first became a team, they built a new "to-do" list at every meeting and never stopped to reflect on what had been done or was still to be done. Now in checking the action plan, when an action is done, the accountability includes stopping and reflecting:

- *How was that accomplished?*
- *Did we get the desired impact? If so, what was it?*
- *Is there more that needs to be done?*
- *What did we learn that will be helpful in our other actions?*

In accountability we usually think about:
- making assignments
- asking for volunteers

To gain an edge, include other accountability issues:

- Be clear about what is expected of each person. Thinking together is not about "being nice" to each other. It means helping each other do thinking together.

  Establish the task ... What is the desired outcome?

  Know the purpose ... Why is this important?

  Be clear about what thinking together takes ... What's needed from us/me?

- Understand and expect people to be "who they are" – not some ideal. *Carrie will not stop pushing for the details. When she pushes for the details, if necessary to promote thinking together, bring it to her attention. Remind her of the purpose and the task at hand. Don't expect her to just "be different."*

- Help people stay focused on the task at hand. *"Remember, we are trying to uncover what we know about this topic."*

- Take time to summarize what was agreed to, who needs to do it and by when.

Getting the summary up on a white board can help clarify what is expected and who will be accountable by when.

- Encourage people to be honest in reporting work performance by providing a non-threatening, supportive climate.
  Set aside time and a "safe place" for accounting for unfinished projects, mistakes, work that has been forgotten, as well as successes and victories. Facilitate any learning that can be gleaned from such situations.
- Help people be accountable by creating scenarios where possibilities can be played out. This can raise unknown questions and may provide an option of "testing" before final implementation.
- Make sure that people experience absolution in the face of outcomes that miss the target. Let the team figure out the next moves and the best way to move forward.
- Gain the needed support so the people critical to the effort are involved.
- Recognize that to make a "to do" list for another person is an unhelpful exercise.

One of Dr. Deming's favorite stories was about accountability. During a seminar he commented, "I got a pair of new shoes." "Did you get a good deal?" a student asked. His reply was, "I can't tell you if it was a good deal until the day they wear out. I can't evaluate if it was a good deal without knowing how long they last."[3]

Thinkabouts in Accountability

Thinkabout

1. If you expect to have more say in what happens, be accountable for helping make it happen.
2. If you expect ownership for a project, be accountable for helping get it done.
3. It you expect to decide your day-to-day priorities, be accountable to customers, peers and the organization.
4. If you expect to be part of decision-making, be accountable for the results.

Methods

Think through what facilitation methods are most appropriate for a given meeting or interaction – brainstorming, grouping ideas, small-group work, action plans, getting everyone involved and using life/work examples to illustrate ideas, and so on.

Be aware when a shift in methods will ease the way to move forward. Possibilities include:

- Early on, set up opportunities for people to express themselves. Only ask questions if you really want to know. Ask with a sincere desire to understand. An inviting style will evoke an open response. An interrogating tone will evoke a defensive response. "Share with us what you are hoping for today." "Give us a quick sense of …"
- Recognize the situation at hand and put it into words (e.g., "It seems the move has us all a bit unsettled. Do we need to take a minute to talk about this?").
- Create a safe zone. Trust your intuitions, your instincts – your sixth sense of things.
- Allow people a chance to pause and think about what is going on (e.g., "Jane has just given us an idea on how to move with this, let's think for a minute about how we can add to this idea."). Reflective techniques communicate your intent. Reflect at strategic points throughout the process. People learn more through reflection than through repetition. When small-group work is completed, ask people to be reflective, and as a group, reflect on small-group reports. Ask others to note where they found the team was on target and where they have questions. Ask people to share key points that "we need to remember."
- Reflect on information presented so you can uncover meaning and implications (e.g., "What came easily as you defined the purpose?" "Where were you struggling?" "Why is purpose so important?").
- Use the dynamics of the small group/large group to enhance participation, generate ideas and move more quickly.
- Decide when to hold "story swap" sessions for sharing stories about what is working and why in order to learn from each other.
- Plan a reflective conversation on how far the team has come. Too often the focus is on what is left to do rather than on what has already been accomplished.

Space

The physical environment creates expectations. For example, going into a room that is messy, chaotic and has a bad odor gives an expectation of a disorganized, unfocused event. Locations can also evoke memories. A space where a particularly joyful, or painful, event occurred, brings back those memories.

Consider space requirements. The configuration and use of space can help or hinder every aspect of working together effectively as illustrated in the following scenario.

Saturday's training session for the high school staff is scheduled for the school cafeteria. When she arrives early to check the space, Josie, the trainer, discovers the room is in shambles. None of the tables are set as she requested and trash and clutter are strewn everywhere. She quickly sets to work to organize the space. Although the space is not as Josie wants by the time the participants arrive, she decides to begin the session on time after all.

Early on it becomes clear that the space is causing chaotic, slipshod thinking. Josie shifts gears and asks for small groups to work on several targeted questions. When the small groups reorganize their individual spaces in order to talk together, the conversations become more animated and focused. The rearrangement of the team spaces brings the whole cafeteria into line with Josie's expectations. The difference in the teams' willingness and eagerness to think together is apparent right away.

Space is crucial in a participatory process. Set the room up so ideas can flow back and forth easily. Keep in mind the size of the room when requesting space for an interaction. In a room that is too small for the work, there is not enough space for people to think effectively and ideas can't get out. On the other hand, in a room that is too large, ideas float off in space and fail to connect or register with people.

To gain an edge, evaluate the space before the meeting:

- Get information on the space in advance and arrive early to reconfigure as needed.
- Clear enough wall space to hang the team's work if appropriate.
- Arrange space for small-group breakouts, if that is anticipated.
- Arrange the tables and chairs so people can see each other most effectively.
- Assess what is needed for people who are participating via teleconference.

Setting up a room so it works for the group is an act of caring for the group and for the interaction. In the ritual of moving chairs and removing or covering distracting pictures, you align your own thinking with the thinking of the group.

To review the T-E-A-M-S environment, see Figure 4, Creating the T-E-A-M-S Environment – recall how crucial the design of time is, the liveliness in events, the clarity in accountability, the appropriateness of innovative methods and the shaping of space for the desired results.

Creating the T-E-A-M-S Environment

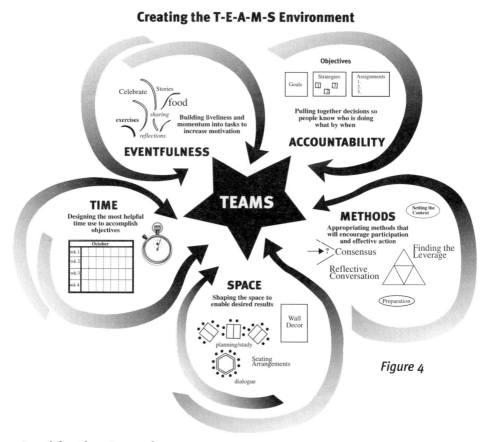

Figure 4

Decide the Agenda

Solidifying the agenda is a culmination of strategic prethinking. Think through each part of the agenda and the role it plays in accomplishing the outcome of the meeting. The following is an example of a traditional printed agenda:

1. Opening context – 5 min.
2. Accomplishments to date – 20 min.
3. Action still needed for completion – 35 min.

4. Timeline and assignments – 45 min.

5. FYI – 7 min.

6. Closing reflection – 8 min.

    • Summary of decisions

    • Reflection on what was accomplished

An agenda is a map of the meeting flow. Drawing a chart of the agenda may help you check out your thinking as it allows you to see how the people involved can achieve the outcome for the interaction. Figure 5 is one way to see the interaction in a picture and experience the flow of time.

Sample Agenda

Opening	Content of Interaction				Closing
	I	II	III	FYI	
Intent know: • actions to date • deadline experience: • have accomplished a lot • confidence **Context** The ABC project was given to us a month ago and we've been asked to complete it in six weeks in order to mesh with other organizational goals. We'd like to draw out a timeline for our work. Can we spend a couple of hours to do this?	**Accomplishments to date** 1. get up list of accomplishments 2. reflect on what has been learned Transition	**Actions still needed** 1. brainstorm 2. organize information 3. name action steps needed 4. reflect on what this means Transition	**Building the timeline with assignments** 1. designate completion date 2. lay out action steps over time 3. make assignments for who will do what by when Transition	**Other info the team needs**	**Reflection**
5 min.	20 min.	35 min.	45 min.	7 min.	8 min.

Outcome: To decide the timeframe and assignments to complete the ABC project.

Figure 5

Once you determine the agenda, create any necessary handouts. Handouts may include the agenda, models, proposals, list of attendees, memo copies, proposed designs, and so on. The key in preparing handouts is design care, relevance, clarity and readability. If you want a handout to be taken seriously, it needs to look like you cared about its preparation.

Thinkabouts in Orchestrating Interactions

1. The group can establish meeting norms at the beginning of a meeting or the person facilitating may suggest some parameters.

2. One of the most helpful rules is: "Only suggestions, no vetoes."

3. Do not make or allow conversation-stopping comments like, "I just don't like that," or "That just won't work." Ask a question so everyone can better understand a person's thinking.

   "Can you say a little more about that so we understand your thinking?"
   "What elements of the proposal don't you like?"
   "Can you help us understand what has led you to this conclusion?"

4. Share concerns and seek alternatives.

   "Now that we understand Butch's perspective better, what are some other perspectives?"

Post-Interaction Thinking

After the interaction, step back and take a second look at what took place. This post-interaction thinking is often overlooked in the press of time. There are four basic reasons for making it a regular part of your wrap-up in conversation with the group:

1. People have an opportunity to review and remember the sequence (flow) of what happened.

2. Participants can see more objectively their relationship to what went on and their reaction to it.

3. Participants get to listen to themselves and others discuss why the interaction was important and how it will make a difference.

4. Everyone can reconfirm the decisions and reaffirm their own commitments to making them happen.

Examples of helpful post-interaction questions include:
   • What actually happened?
   • What did we do, see, hear?
   • Who was there?

- Where were you excited, intrigued, concerned, worried?
- What was important for you, for the team? Why?
- What difference would it make if (authority figures) weren't there?
- What decisions did we make?
- What did we discover about the people involved?
- What worked and why … what did not work and why?
- What did we learn that will make a difference in what we are doing?
- What next?
    - So what?
    - How do our learnings inform what needs to happen next?
    - What are the priorities for the next steps?
    - Who is responsible for the next steps?
    - When do we expect these next steps to happen?

Weave the Silver Thread

The silver thread is the primary theme that knits an interaction together. It ties all parts of the agenda together and constantly lets people know what we are doing and why. The silver thread is most often carried through reflective questions that ask people to stop and think about what is going on.

A thread of thought (the silver thread) that ties an event and activity to the purpose and mission of the group helps people make sense of what is happening.

As you are preparing, ask yourself:
"What is the primary theme (silver thread) that runs through the meeting or event?"
"What reflective questions will emphasize the silver thread?"
"What do we need in the meeting or interaction environment to reflect the silver thread?"

For example, for a meeting whose intent was to bring "turf"-bound parts of a team together, the silver thread might be "learning to work together." The silver thread could be reinforced and show up in the questions asked, "What have we learned today about working together? How is this meeting helping us work better together?" This enables people to see their ups and downs within the framework of a journey rather than random activities that make no sense.

- We started (or will start) here ...
- The important steps (process or events) have (or will be) ...
- We are now here ...
- We are going there ...
- It is like a ...

Tying issues and situations together with a silver thread weaves a common sense of identity and purpose.

The charts in Figures 6a and 6b summarize the process for orchestrating interactions.

Process for Orchestrating Interactions

Strategic Assessment

 Strategically assess if the outcome is realistic

- What is the outcome's relevant history?

- What is going on now?

- As you listened to people, what were their expectations?

- What support is there for this outcome?

You are now ready to ask the question, "Is this outcome realistic?"
If it is, move to the second step.
If it isn't, ask yourself and others what is needed to make it realistic ... or forget the whole idea.

 Project how the outcome will be accomplished

- What are the outcome's biggest challenges?

- Where is this outcome in the organization's priority list?

- How much authority will this outcome require to be successful?

- Who are the critical people who need to be involved?

Can you say with confidence that all the bases have been touched in projecting what it will take to meet this outcome? If the answer is yes, move to Intentional Scripting. If no, review your work and make adjustments.

Your picture is not complete until you talk to people who will be involved.

Figure 6a

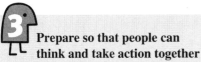
Intentional Scripting

Prepare so that people can think and take action together

- Decide the intent

- Create the context

- Think about the environment

    – Work out a **T**imeframe

    – Consider the **E**ventfulness

    – Decide how **A**ccountability will be built into the process

    – Decide the appropriate **M**ethods

    – Design the creative use of **S**pace

Weave the Silver Thread

- What is the primary theme (silver thread) that runs through the event?

- What reflective questions will emphasize the silver thread?

- What needs to be printed on the agenda to drive home the silver thread?

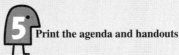
Print the agenda and handouts

Your preparation is not finished until you have checked it out with the people who will be involved.

Figure 6b

Even with the most careful prethinking and preparation, a group may move in an unexpected (perhaps creative) direction. Think through possible "what ifs?" beforehand. This strengthens your intentionality and allows you to be present in the interaction rather than thinking about what you are doing next. If you have done the prethinking stage carefully, it will be easier to adapt and adjust.

"Each moment presents a new situation in which we are sensitive, aware, deciding, and relating/responding."
– Basil Sharp[4]

Generate Reflection

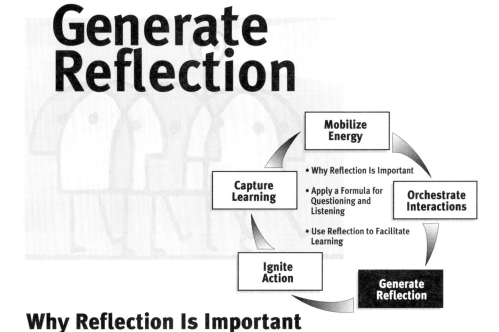

Mobilize Energy

- Why Reflection Is Important
- Apply a Formula for Questioning and Listening
- Use Reflection to Facilitate Learning

Capture Learning

Orchestrate Interactions

Ignite Action

Generate Reflection

Why Reflection Is Important

"When group members have time to reflect, they see more clearly what is essential in themselves and others."
– John Heider[1]

The word "reflection" used to conjure up images of a person sitting cross-legged, alone, apparently lost in deep thought. Today the concept of reflection has come off the mountain and into the workplace. "In the knowledge economy, the most important work is conversation (reflecting together) and creating trust is the manager's most important job," says Alan Webber.[2] "Stop talking and get to work!" is being replaced by "Start talking and get to work!" The reflective process slows things down so we observe and experience what is going on to gain a new perspective. Conversations trigger the growth of knowledge – questions are the mode and dialogue is the medium.

Shifts in our ways of thinking and interacting are a given in this time of constant change. Figure 1 (page 86) recaps some of these shifts that are calling for us to reflect together.

Shifts in Ways of Thinking and Interacting

Shifting	
from	**to**
someone else is in charge	we create and invent the future
hoarding information	sharing information
controlling people	releasing imagination
seeing detail complexity	seeing dynamical complexity
styles that suppress and	styles that facilitate and
intimidate	empower

Figure 1

Start Talking and Get to Work

"I know you believe you understand what you think I said, but I'm not sure you realize what you heard is not what I meant."
– Anonymous

Too often in communication, positioning oneself takes precedence over striving to understand; the person talking is being critical rather than creative; there is more telling than asking. In these situations, the person communicating may not know how to help people think things through together.

Overheard in the cafeteria at a manufacturing plant: "Communication is the key. If people would just communicate with each other and not make assumptions 50 percent of our problems would be solved."

In conversation "today's knowledge workers discover what they know, share it with their colleagues and in the process create new knowledge for the organization," explains Alan Webber.[3] Reflective conversation encourages new thinking. Reflective tools give you intention and direction. Use reflective conversation to:

- generate new ideas
- ponder experiences
- get smarter
- give meaning to information
- transfer learning to other tasks
- test the waters with mindful exploration

Our beliefs shape the realities we experience. According to David Bohm,[4] it is through dialogue that "a new kind of mind begins to come into being based on the development of common meaning." Through dialogue people work together to understand individual assumptions as well as collective beliefs.

At first, using reflective tools may seem risky for several reasons, including:

- Fear of losing control:
  - afraid we won't be able to respond to an answer
  - unsure of the group's attitude
- Lack of self-confidence:
  - don't want to appear stupid or dumb
  - afraid no one will answer
- Limited time:
  - "it is too close to lunch or break"
  - "questions take too much time"

The facilitative skills with which you generate reflection are means for overcoming these communication barriers. The following seven ways can help you open up dialogue using reflective conversations.

1. Ask open-ended questions so people can stop and think – "How might we look at this another way?"
2. Sequence questions so people's thinking moves from surfacing facts, through facing emotions to examining implications and making decisions – "What do you see? ⟶ Where have you seen that before? ⟶ What does it mean? ⟶ What will it do for us?"
3. Suggest a new context – "Let's take a minute to look at this from the perspective of the customer. What differences will that make?"
4. Pause after important comments to give people time to decide what they think is important – "This part of the proposal seems important to us" – pause before further comment.
5. Stir the thinking behind what is said – "Help us understand." "A helpful image, can you say more?" "Jordan has reminded us of ..."
6. Ask for the relevance of a statement to the issue at hand – "What is important in this?" "How does this help us serve our customers?" "What assumptions are being made here?"
7. Recognize experience – "You know a lot about this already, let's pick up on how to do this in this particular situation."

Both advocating your position and allowing dialogue are important.

People are more schooled in advocacy (telling) and not so well adept at reflective dialogue (asking). Telling conveys information, ideas, thoughts, decision and directions. Asking uncovers others' insights, deepens thinking and guides a group to a decision together.

Use advocacy to	Use dialogue to
• make a point	• understand a point
• convince others	• build common ground
• push a particular perspective	• explore options
• sell a position	• think it through together
• get your point of view on the table	• get the thinking behind views on the table

Frame a New Point of Reference

Using dialogue in a reflective conversation can frame a new point of reference for thinking together. The power of personal reflection applied to groups can energize the organization by:

1. Clarifying shared values in order to agree on what is important, encourage individual integrity and provide motivation for engagement.
2. Developing innovative methods in order to learn from each other, generate practical knowledge and tap people's creativity.
3. Ensuring information access to let people assume a new level of responsibility and be meaningfully engaged in communication and action.

Apply a Formula for Questioning and Listening

"Assumptions affect observation. Observation breeds Conviction. Conviction produces Experience. Experience generates Behavior, which in turn, confirms Assumptions."
– Anthony de Mello[5]

Tap into the Natural Thinking Process

There is an art to asking effective questions. The key lies in knowing the questions to ask, the sequence of asking and how to listen to the answers. Effective questions encourage

Facilitative Approach

people to operate beyond emotions, immediacies, generalities or "we've always done it this way." Sequencing questions and effective listening wake people up to possibility and responsibility.

>*The team has been having regular meetings ever since its formation. The meetings seem a waste of time. People just talk at each other. No one listens. No one leads, and everyone is anxious to get back to work.*
>
>*One day one of the team members, Susie, requests permission to ask some questions if people will answer one at a time. This seems to be as good a way as any to spend the time, so people quiet down and give Susie their attention.*
>
>*Susie selects Project X from the team's agenda and explains that it might help to back up and find out where they are. She deliberately slows the pace and quiets her tone so people have to lean forward to catch what she is saying. The cacophony stops. The discord begins to disappear.*
>
>*Susie asks a series of questions to discover the facts and she records each on the flip chart exactly as it is said. Then she records various feelings, experiences and associations. People are surprised as they listen and hear the others. This mix of all the "I" thinking, the facts and experiences vastly enlarges the context.*
>
>*A new possibility, shifting to "we" thinking, now exists because each person has been heard. The energy level and attention rise as solutions bubble forth, each acknowledged by Susie. Somehow Susie has created a climate in which divergent views are being invited.*
>
>*As the meeting progresses, team members realize that their individual ideas ("I" thinking) have developed into the team's thinking ("we" thinking). At the end of the meeting Susie helps the team reflect on what happened to change the tone of the meeting. There was:*
>   - *a new level of listening*
>   - *a review of the ground previously covered*
>   - *a plan of action*
>   - *next steps*
>   - *a summary of what had happened during the meeting*
>
>*The team members realize that "real work" has happened.*

What can a question do that an answer cannot? A question invites a response, makes you think, takes thinking to a deeper level, invites participation and helps people consider their preferred thinking patterns. Questions help you revisit what you thought you knew and then rethink your position.

Conversation inspires concrete action

A formula for asking questions and listening for answers, based on our natural thinking process, will facilitate a conversation that can generate new knowledge and, ultimately, action.

Why a formula for questions and for listening? Focused, sequenced questioning collects data, responds to it and forms meaning and knowledge. We live in two worlds – the world of data and the world of meaning. Data overwhelm us and isolate us, whereas meaning enlightens and connects us. Knowledge in turn flows from meaning. In an age of information explosion, knowledge becomes increasingly crucial as organizations measure their intellectual capital.

In our mind's natural reflective process we:

1. absorb raw data – our brains take in sensory information – the facts
2. relate to these data – we color the sensory information with our experiences, associations and feelings
3. interpret the data to reveal implications
4. apply what we have learned (using the above) to make a decision

In brief, our natural reflective process is an FFID (facts, feelings, implications, decision) process (see Figure 2). To illustrate, think about going through the checkout lines at the grocery store:

1. You take in facts and data about the situation:

    Five checkout stands are open, at least two people in each line.
    Checkout stand 3 (the fast lane) is moving really slowly.

2. You relate to these facts through feelings and experiences:

    It is frustrating when people with more than fifteen items use the fast lane. I like the person running register 7; she is always courteous.

3. You interpret the facts and how you relate to them in order to determine the implications and significance:

    If I go to register 7, I'll be third in line – about where I'd be at any of the registers.

4. Finally, you make a decision based on these facts, feelings and implications:

    I go to the line at register 7.

Natural Thinking Process

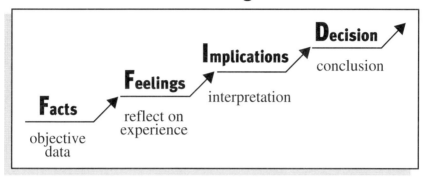

Figure 2

Guide Reflection with "I" Thinking Plus "We" Thinking

Too often we ask, "What do you think of the proposal?" This is asking an interpretation question first. When this happens, only a portion of the natural thinking process is used. We hear individual opinions before we hear any facts and feelings. When facts and feelings are taken into account, the group can move beyond opinions to interpretations, implications and decisions. For example:

"What words or phrases caught your attention in the proposal?" (facts)

"What is in the proposal?" (facts)

"What parts of the proposal seem on target to you?" (feelings)

"Which parts concern you?" (feelings)

This is an example of "I" thinking. The objective nature of facts reveals what individuals have noticed in the proposal. Hearing from several people allows a broader "remembering" of the proposal's contents. The reflective level of feelings surfaces emotions and experiences. When ignored, emotions and feelings often jeopardize decisions.

The group's thinking ("We" thinking) builds on what individuals have expressed. Implications questions help to develop a common interpretation, which allows the group to create a framework for a joint decision.

"As you listened to each other, what appears to be the key issues this proposal addresses?" (implications)

"Taking into account some of our concerns, how will this proposal affect the work of our team?" (implications)

"What changes do we want to recommend?" (decision)

The value of "I" thinking:
- Reviews individuals' facts so everyone has a common picture
- Hears individuals' perceptions of the facts
- Allows individuals to express feelings and experiences so decisions are strengthened

The value of "We" thinking:
- Generates new, original ideas
- Shifts the focus from individuals to the understanding of the group
- Builds trust and support in the group
- Ensures a supported group decision

The following are some common behaviors you will run into when helping people think together.
- Stating and selling an opinion without sharing the thinking. "I am sure the best software for us to buy is ..."
- People bringing hidden agendas which they are prepared to defend. "Our team can do this event without help from any of the other teams."
- Someone asks a question with the answer "attached."
    "There is agreement, isn't there?"
    "It is pretty obvious, isn't it?"

Facilitative Response

True dialogue and reflection can only happen when issues are "on the table." Thinking and issues that remain unspoken block the possibility of thinking together.
- Ask the reflective questions that get the thinking on the table so thinking together can happen.
    "What have we heard the staff say about the software?"
    "What questions of clarity do you have?"
    "Can you help us understand what you heard or read that led you to that conclusion?"
- Ask the reflective questions that get the agendas on the table and help people think together about the implications and action that follow.
    "What additional information do we need to be effective in implementation?"
    "As you think about implementing the change, what will be our biggest challenge and why?"
    "What perspective do we need to keep here and why?"

- Ask an open-ended reflective question that elicits the thinking behind the answer.

   "What have you heard us say that suggests that is the way to go?"

Based on the natural thinking process, the Conversation Formula captures the way we think in a structured flow of questions. Use this formula in various types of conversations, from group problem-solving to quick, check-it-out, communications. For example,

"What room do you have for the meeting?" (*facts*)

"Have you used that room before? How well does it work?" (*feelings*)

"How can we use the space to the greatest advantage?" (*implications*)

"What do we need to do to get it ready?" (*decision*)

Two basic assumptions allow the FFID formula for questions to work:
- Every person has a perspective that needs to be listened to and honored
- Questions are more powerful than answers

Figure 3 (page 94) recaps the natural thinking process and demonstrates the sequencing of questions in the Conversation Formula.

If one or more levels are left out of the process, the decision will not be as effective as it could be. For example, sometimes we assume the objective data are obvious so it is difficult to ask for them. Figure 4 (page 95) illustrates some of the potential results when one of the levels is omitted.

Knowledge grows out of conversations that use all four levels. Here is an example of using the FFID formula in a performance debriefing conversation.

"I know you are involved in a special project for the department. Will you describe one thing about the job you have been doing?" (**Facts** question asks for data on what the person has been doing.)

"What have been your accomplishments and challenges?" (**Feelings** question triggers a reflection on what is causing the results.)

"What are you hoping to accomplish as you continue this project?" (**Implications** question draws out new understandings about what is going on.)

"What do you intend for your next steps?" (**Decision** question helps everyone be more effective by stating resolve for action.)

Much has been learned in recent years about how the human brain functions. Figure 5 describes the development of the human brain's thinking

Conversation Formula
Sequencing Questions to Reach a Decision

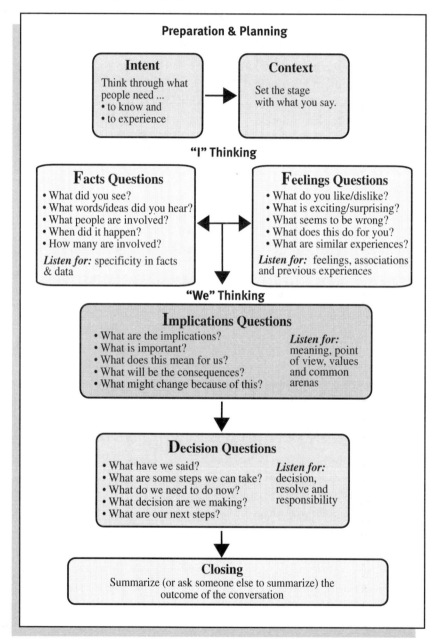

Preparation & Planning

Intent
Think through what
people need ...
• to know and
• to experience

Context
Set the stage
with what you say.

"I" Thinking

Facts Questions
• What did you see?
• What words/ideas did you hear?
• What people are involved?
• When did it happen?
• How many are involved?

Listen for: specificity in facts
& data

Feelings Questions
• What do you like/dislike?
• What is exciting/surprising?
• What seems to be wrong?
• What does this do for you?
• What are similar experiences?

Listen for: feelings, associations
and previous experiences

"We" Thinking

Implications Questions
• What are the implications?
• What is important?
• What does this mean for us?
• What will be the consequences?
• What might change because of this?

Listen for:
meaning, point
of view, values
and common
arenas

Decision Questions
• What have we said?
• What are some steps we can take?
• What do we need to do now?
• What decision are we making?
• What are our next steps?

Listen for:
decision,
resolve and
responsibility

Closing
Summarize (or ask someone else to summarize) the
outcome of the conversation

Figure 3

What Happens When We Skip a Level

___X___ + Feelings + Implications + Decision =	Decision without data; let's hope it was a "no brainer."
Facts + ___X___ + Implications + Decision =	Decision is made without feeling or experience; no passion or ownership.
Facts + Feelings + ___X___ + Decision =	Decision is made without analysis; the "emotional buy."
Facts + Feelings + Implications + ___X___ =	There is no decision, but a great discussion; the "group think."
Facts + Feelings + Implications + Decision =	Firm decision is made based on data, feelings, implications and conclusions.

Figure 4

process in the evolutionary and maturation processes, illustrating the development of our natural thinking process.

The FFID Conversation Formula helps people be smarter as they reflect consciously at all levels. Sequenced questions move the thinking from one level to the next, challenging assumptions along the way.

The Brain's Thinking Process[6]

Brain research has shown that neurologically the entire animal kingdom, down to the earthworm, takes in some or all sensory input consciously or unconsciously. We see, hear, feel, taste, and smell. This relates to the first category of gathering facts. People (and other animals) react to sensory input. Dogs associate with their master's smell; infants recognize their mother among other women. This relates to the category of feelings, experiences, associations.

The right hemisphere of the brain sorts out sensory input (*facts* and *feelings*) and the left hemisphere of the brain interprets and labels (*implications*). When a child can determine, "that's good" applied to specific foods, toys or people, the child uses feelings to interpret data (*implications*).

The frontal part of the brain is the last to develop. This is the place where *decisions* with consequences are made. This is why teens often make foolish decisions with no thought for consequences. People often jump to conclusions and opinions without looking at the sensory input, feelings and implications.

Figure 5

95

Invite Reflection

**"In knowledge work, the first question is 'What should you be doing?'
Not how. There is very little joy in heaven or on earth over an
engineering department that, with great zeal, great expertise, and
great diligence, produces drawings for the wrong product. 'What you
should do,' is the first question when you deal with the productivity of
knowledge. It's a very difficult question, but an important one."
– Peter Drucker[7]**

Reflection is critical both for motivation and for verifying results. Ask the
questions that are needed, and use an inviting style to create comfort and trust.
In creating an inviting style rely on:

- Context: Establish why generating reflective thinking is important –
  remember to think through the desired outcome and intent. Your context
  sets the stage.
- FFID sequence: This is the essence of thinking together. When people give
  a knowledgeable opinion, they have already listened to each other's facts
  and feelings. Without the specific sequence, conversation becomes a battle
  of opinions in a negative atmosphere, which undermines the trust that is
  essential to an open, inviting dialogue.
- When formulating questions, keep in mind:
  - Make the facts question(s) easy to answer.
    "What is one thing you remember from the presentation?" vs.
    "What do you remember being said?"
  - Feelings questions are about more than emotions. Include
    questions about associations and experiences, such as "Has
    anyone experienced this before? Please share what happened."
  - Implication questions have a direct relationship to the intent; for
    example, "As you have listened to what we've said, what would be
    some of the consequences of not implementing the new policy?"

*Virgil's team has just finished a three-month project. He knows the
lessons learned from this project will be helpful as the team looks toward a
new challenge. The problem is, there is a push to keep moving forward.*

Nevertheless, Virgil decides to lead a reflective conversation with the team to discover what they learned and what they feel good about.

Virgil sets the stage. "Before we begin this new project, I'd like to take a few minutes to think about what we learned from the last project and how we can use those lessons to help us on our next assignment. Are you willing to try this out?"

When team members say "OK," he is ready to go. (If they didn't say OK, he would have asked some reflective "what did we learn in that last project?" questions in planning the new project.)

"Think about one thing you remember about this last project. Will someone volunteer to share?" Virgil encourages several people to respond and listens as people recreate the events of the project. (Facts)

Then he asks, "Where did we have successes and why?"

"Where did we have struggles and why?" (Listen for people's Feelings and experiences.)

"What did we learn?" (Listen for Implications, for the meaning.)

"How can we apply what we've learned to this new effort?"

When team members have no comment, Virgil doesn't force it. Instead he moves on looking for ways to encourage reflection as they talk about the next project.

"What experiences from our past work might help us with this?"

"How does this relate to what we did on the last project?"

"Can someone help me see how we can avoid that issue again?"

Thinkabouts for Asking Questions That Invite Reflection

Thinkabout

1. Keep questions open-ended.

   For example, by asking such questions as, "What concerns you about this plan?" vs. "Are you concerned about this plan?" (close-ended), you'll spark more thinking and learn a lot more. If you do ask a closed-ended question, you can open it back up by adding "why or why not?" to the end of the question.

2. Anchor questions with a mini-context.

   Questions can sound abrupt when there is no context. In many instances a full context is not needed; a mini-context is usually enough.

   "In light of our efforts to understand what this situation requires, help us understand your perspective. When you say, 'interface more with the customer,' what do you mean?" rather than "What do you mean by that?"

"It helps us all to see value if we can try and estimate the impact an action might have. Could you describe what difference your proposed action might make?" rather than "What difference will that make?"

3. Reset the context as necessary to maintain focus.

"It is easy to jump to a decision here. We started out committed to reviewing all the data first. Are there additional facts we need to consider?"

4. Ask only one question at a time and be comfortable with silence. Ask a question and then be quiet. People need time to process and think. This seems simple but can be hard. Don't be tempted to keep asking questions so "someone will surely answer."

5. Draw out different perspectives and points of view to enrich the thinking. "What's another perspective? Someone else, please share what you are thinking."

6. Recap and summarize so everyone can track the group's thinking or ask for others to recap and summarize.

"What have we said that is important?" "Stepping back, how would you summarize the key points we've talked about?"

7. Use outcome and intent to keep your questions focused.

For example, assume the outcome is to reach a decision about the proposal. The intent is for team members to understand the proposal and its relevance and to experience deciding together. Another set of questions about the proposal might include, "What was one point in the proposal?" "Somebody else, what was another point?" "What in the proposal was of concern?" "Where did you get excited about the possibility of this?" "As you think about what we've said, what is the relevance of this proposal to our work?" "What would make it more relevant and why?" "What are we saying is the next step?" "What have we decided?"

In suggesting that one requirement in an information-based organization is that everyone take responsibility for information, Peter Drucker recommends that we ask:

- "Who depends on me for information?"
- "And on whom do I depend?"[8]

Reflective Learning

For help in generating reflection, the Appendix includes:
- the history of the development of the Conversation Formula
- a chart on which you can practice writing out questions for a particular situation
- additional sample conversations

Listen with Intent

In talk we send out messages. In listening we receive messages. And in conversation we do both. It is an exchange – sending and receiving, a way of getting inside another's thinking.

In any interaction the tone and style we use communicate intent. Six percent of communication takes place verbally, 12 percent from tone of voice and 82 percent is nonverbal! When there is a difference between what is said and what body language implies, your body language communicates nonverbally no matter what you say.[9]

> **Essential in the communication process is the belief in and respect for people's capacity to contribute.**

When talking together, there is a tendency in our fast-paced culture to skip over the *facts* in a situation. Plus, you only need one bad experience in dealing with people's emotions to know why *feelings* and experiences are often not part of a conversation. *Implications* are often the first thing out of people's mouths. Everyone wants to tell you his or her perspective. Finally, talking for talking's sake might be fun but it doesn't get the job done. Listen for the *decision* that brings the conversation to a resolution or close. These insights provide four listening posts:
- listening for facts
- listening for feelings
- listening for implications
- listening for a decision

Communication is most effective when you use these four unique listening posts. They are activated by questions that demonstrate active listening and build upon the levels of the natural thinking process discussed earlier.

Listening Post #1 – Facts

What do facts sound like?
- Information – deadlines, key points, etc.
- Data – reports, numbers, etc.
- What was heard, seen, touched, smelled
- Definitions

Questions that extract the facts:
"What data are available?"
"What do we know about this?"
"What was one point being made?"
"When you use the term 'client-focused,' what pictures come to mind?"
"Which deadlines did we meet? Which ones did we miss?"
"What did you hear the staff say?"

Thinkabouts – Listening for Facts

Thinkabout

1. Pay attention to the specificity in the answers – what people see, hear, taste, smell.
2. Often an opinion is voiced in response to a facts question. Follow up with a question that reveals what is behind the opinion, "What did you observe that shaped your response?"

Listening Post #2 – Feelings, Experiences, Associations

What do feelings and experiences sound like?
- Likes/dislikes
- Previous experiences and associations
- Points of concern/excitement
- Joys and disappointments

Questions that surface feelings and experiences include:
"What do you like/dislike?"
"What similar experiences have you had?"
"What about this is familiar/unfamiliar?"
"What is exciting/disturbing?"
"What about this is difficult/easy?"
"What worked well? What didn't work as well?"
"How do you find yourself reacting to this?"

Thinkabouts – Listening for Feelings

1. Feelings and associations combined with facts yield a rich pool of insights on which to base implications and decisions.

2. Emotions are powerful and therefore can get the conversation off track. When this happens, restate the focus of the conversation.

3. When the time seems right, remind everyone that you will be moving past facts and feelings to implications and decision (the third and fourth listening posts). For example, you may say "We've heard much of our individual thinking, let's see what we can make of it all."

Listening Post #3 – Implications

What do implications sound like?
- Insights that reflect the intent
- Consequences
- The reason something is important
- The meaning for the group

Questions that draw implications from the group's thinking include:

"What will be different?"

"What are we trying to communicate?"

"What changes do we need to make to meet these guidelines?"

"Thinking about all that has been said, what is one option?"

"From what we've heard, what is one consequence of not doing anything?"

"As you think about what has been said, what might change?"

"What values do we need to hold as we move forward with this?"

Thinkabouts – Listening for Implications

1. Jumping to an opinion or conclusion before hearing facts and feelings does not take into account the individual thinking in the group.

2. The most time may be spent in this part of the conversation as you are asking for deeper thinking.

3. Listen for the meaning and purpose that people give to the situation.

4. Listen for the thinking behind people's statements as they interpret what they have heard from the group.
5. Listen for implications that are drawn from what everyone has said versus solely from one person's opinion

Listening Post #4 – Decisions

What does decision sound like?
- Commitment
- Next steps
- Conclusions
- Bringing to a close

Questions that help craft the statement of a decision include:

"What have we said?"

"What are some steps we can take?"

"What do we need to do next?"

"Who needs to take responsibility for what?"

"How soon do we want to start?"

"If you were to summarize what we need, what would you say?"

Thinkabouts – Listening for Decisions

1. A decision "not to decide" is a decision.
2. Talking with commitment doesn't get the job done.
3. It is important to listen for the decision that brings the conversation to a resolution or close.

Thinkabout

Listen with a Third Ear

Listen "between the lines" for the listening posts that are said and left unsaid, or unexplained. Be aware of the nuances that mask unexpressed emotions. Give feedback on feelings as well as facts, "Is this alright for you or is it still bothering you?"

Hearing what is being said and not said requires concentrating on the spoken words as well as observing nonverbal signals, that is, tone, body language and gestures. Let all your senses take in information.

- Pick up on the significance that lies behind people's words. Ask about negatively phrased comments to reveal the underlying insight. Clarify generalizations, "What have you seen that makes you say, 'All of them do'?"

- Listen for the issue behind the issue, "This seems to be hard to discuss. Why do you think that is?"
- Hear deeper patterns of meaning. Sort out the connections and interpretations. "When you say that, are you worried about the work he did last month or thinking about this new project?"
- Take into account the context and situation of the speaker. For example, is it a contribution, part of a complaint, or more brainstorming.
- Strive to understand and listen for the message instead of thinking about what you'll say next. Allow silence as you stay focused on the speaker. Allow time for thinking, evaluating and analyzing.
- Confirm your understanding by repeating conversationally what you think the speaker has said, "What I understand you are saying is ..." Ask about assumptions that you think you hear.

Use Reflection to Facilitate Learning

"It is becoming clear that the more information we amass, the more important context and meaning become."
– Wm. Van Dusen Wishard[10]

Change Data and Information into Knowledge

How-to Action

Changing the style of behavior and interactions in the workplace to be responsive to today's marketplace realities requires continuous learning. One of the struggles of being a learning organization is to convert facts and data to information and then to knowledge. The leadership challenge is to grow knowledge in the organization using a facilitative approach. Why is it difficult to share knowledge? One of the prime reasons is that, without realizing it, people inject barriers into their communication. A barrier is anything that blocks the meaning in the communication. I may hear what you are saying, but I don't hear what you mean. I have judgments or fears that block me from getting your meaning.

Facts and data are the basic building blocks, but we need to convert them to information to make sense and give meaning. Knowledge, in turn, is information presented in usable patterns that can improve our work and living by helping us work smarter. The reflective process is a way to convert data into knowledge, as shown in Figure 6.

Reflective Process

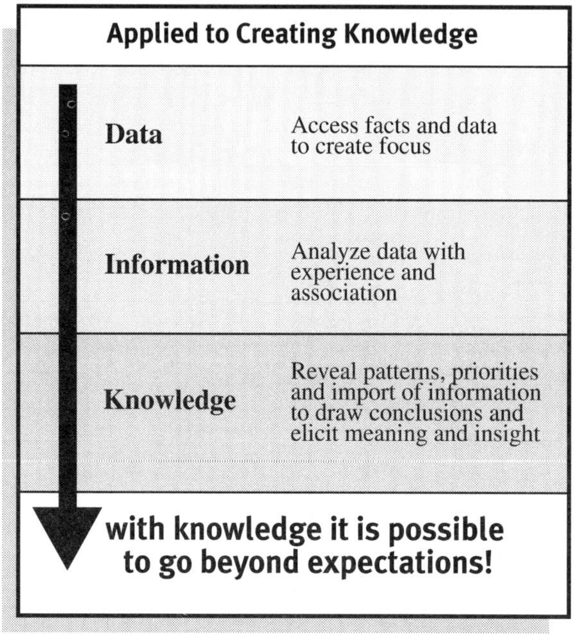

Applied to Creating Knowledge	
Data	Access facts and data to create focus
Information	Analyze data with experience and association
Knowledge	Reveal patterns, priorities and import of information to draw conclusions and elicit meaning and insight

with knowledge it is possible to go beyond expectations!

Figure 6

"Without context, emotions, or patterns, knowledge is considered meaningless. There is a tendency to try to form some kind of meaningful pattern out of our learning – this process seems innate," states Eric Jensen.[11] Together we can:

- Develop a compelling purpose/story about what needs to be done.
- Create a pool of thought where each individual contributes unique thinking.
- Spark reflection that seeks understanding and uncovers insights.
- Encourage excitement to build by adding to the pool of thought not owning the thinking.
- Link minds to develop relevant learning and knowledge.

Release "Out-of-the-Box" Thinking

"As I see it, our precarious position at the top of the competitiveness heap will be sustained only by tapping the imagination of every worker (and student)."
– Tom Peters[12]

Often we are busy thinking about our own to-do lists rather than the project being discussed. Without innovative methods that invite a different level of thinking, we may not be open to think about ways we can participate.

A group planning a major project is looking at the activities for the next two months. They have numerous details to handle before the major event.

As the conversation focuses on who is going to do what, the energy level drops; there are longer and longer silences and a definite shift in body language. Several people push back from the table. A few are studying their calendars. A side conversation springs up in a corner of the room. Suddenly extraneous things seem more important than the specifics of the upcoming event.

In response to this behavior, the facilitator shifts the conversation from detailed activities back to the overview of the planned event. "Let's look at this event again and share our expectations for it." As people talk, she writes their exact words on a flip chart.

The facilitator asks, "What is important about these expectations?" "Too time-consuming. I don't see how we can possibly get it all done," says one. "I'm tired just thinking about it. My calendar is already full," answers another.

The facilitator asks each person to write his or her personal appointments and activities on an eight-week calendar on the wall. This establishes a context in which each person's contribution to the project is seen as valued and balanced with respect for other commitments.

The group then works with the calendar, creating innovative ways to get things done. For example, people see different ways to clump activities together, changing the timeline for accomplishing tasks. By the time the planning session is over, participants have shifted from protecting their own agendas to sharing ways to prepare for the event.

As a result, energy returns to the room, people are on their feet moving things around on the calendar. A stalemate has shifted to a rainbow of creativity.

A group planning an event or project needs a way to see the big picture as well as the individual perspectives present. It is hard for a group to think with the same pictures in their heads. Ask six people to report on an accident they observed and their descriptions often sound like six totally different events. Each person thinks, "What I saw and heard is correct." Each perspective is important. When all perspectives are put together, we have the opportunity to think beyond the picture in any one person's head. Shifting from a focus on "my ideas" to creating and reflecting on common ideas gives people a chance to think outside the box.

**Thinking together occurs when people sense an open,
curious environment in which they are challenged and affirmed.**

To encourage out-of-the-box thinking, you may need to: (a) generate new ideas – to explore ideas that can trigger previously unthought-of insights; (b) explore alternative options – to discover roads that are unfamiliar and challenging; and/or (c) offer demanding tasks – to push individuals beyond where they had thought of going in order to discover new talents and skills.

Generate new ideas by asking:
- *Reflective questions:* "Is that the same as … ?" "How is that different from …?" "How could we slant that to fit the situation?"
- *Predicting questions:* "Let's look at this from the perspective of the customer (office, marketing, etc.)." "What differences will that make?"
- *Meaning questions:* "What is important in this?" "How does this help us serve our customers?" "What assumptions are we making here?" "What did we discover in this that we might not have thought of before?" Display cartoons, wall art, and slogans to offer a new perspective on things.

Explore alternative options by asking:
- *Exploratory questions:* "How might we look at this another way?" "What do you want here? And how will you know when you have it?" "Which way should we go? And what are the implications if we do?"

- *Purpose questions:* "How does this fit in light of all the alternatives?" "How does this make sense in terms of all the choices?"
- *Comparison questions:* "What are others doing?" "How has our competition solved this?"

Offer demanding tasks that tap into the capacities of those involved by asking:

- *Experience questions:* "Since you have experience in this, what would you do?" "Drawing on your own experience, what could be a new direction?"
- *Application questions:* "How can we use this?" "Where would these show up in everyday activities?"
- *Implication questions:* "If we begin immediately, what might go right, what might go wrong?" "Imagining that we have done this for three months, what are the consequences? How will your work change if you accomplish this in six weeks?"
- *Commitment questions:* "Because of your experience with___, would you be willing to do this?" "Who will volunteer for this project?" "Here is a new job that fits well within your capacity." "How can you fit ___ into your schedule?"

Even when the work environment is restrictive, you can stimulate reflection by asking:

"What is important here?"

"Can someone remind me of the purpose?"

"How does this help us serve our customers?"

"What assumptions are we making here?"

To value the creative (over the critical) and build on each other's ideas:

1. **Believe in your own and the team's creative abilities.** Recognize all contributions, "Thank you, Barbara, for that idea. What are additional ways we could do that?" Creativity comes when you join different ideas to form a new insight. Share your thinking, listen to others and reflect on what you are hearing.
2. **Set the atmosphere.** It is hard to be creative when colleagues are being negative. Build on, rather than tear down, what others are contributing. "How might we expand on Michael's insight?" Ask people to offer an alternative model instead of criticizing what was proposed.
3. **Fire up passion.** Remind yourself and others of the why of their efforts. Link individual ideas to the big picture.

4. **Draw on available resources.** Share your own facts and feelings/experiences to build on. Listen to others. Bring in new perspectives. Uncover the insights by asking for the implications.

5. **Use creative tension.** Tension is part of the creative process. Use the principle of creative tension to get things done (refer to page 122). Tension is the energy for change, tension generates power, as rich discussions flow from facts and feelings leading often to innovative breakthroughs. Another tension between what exists now, the present, and what is needed in the future provides power for innovation.

   - Keep future possibilities and the reality of the present in front of the team, envisioning possibilities and facing realities.
   - When thinking gets bogged down in the present situation, revisit possibility; identify the blocks in the present situation so the future can become reality.

6. **Allow for time.** It takes time to create new insights and knowledge. Provide learning opportunities and don't feel rushed.

Reflect with Questions to Trigger Insights

As you work to encourage out-of-the-box thinking, dialogue may bog down and you are looking for ways to trigger insights. Have you found yourself in a meeting, conversation or interaction thinking:

"I need to know more."

"I wonder what he means by that?"

"I am not clear about what was just said."

"I wish they would share more about what they are thinking."

"Does anyone else see the connection between this and what we did last week?"

"Would a new perspective help here?"

Sometimes conversations are stifled by what others do or say, or by what they don't say. A reflective question can reopen the conversation.

Use the FFID (facts, feelings, implications, decision) formula as a roadmap for creating questions. Keep in mind that often what you plan does not play out in the heat of the moment. When things don't go according to plan, listen carefully to people's responses and ask reflective follow-up questions. An easy-to-remember trigger is: **C P R**, Please (Clarifying, Probing, Relating,

Predicting). Remember, it is not just the words, but also the tone (inviting) and context (working together to plan, solve problems or arrive at a decision) that trigger insights.

Clarifying questions – Ask for clarity by following up on a comment that might be misunderstood or have multiple meanings.

"When you use the term 'partnering,' what are you referring to?"

"Can you say a little more about what you mean?"

"What did you hear them say?" (Gesturing to the whole group rather than to one person keeps the question positive rather than negative.)

"Would someone summarize what you have heard being said?"

Probing questions – Probe to uncover more specificity as a follow-up on a vague or incomplete comment.

"What other information would clarify that?"

"What needs to change and why?"

"What are you concerned about and why?"

"This seems like a difficult topic for us, why is that?

Relating questions – Connect topics or people to one another.

"How does this relate to what we did last week?"

"What is the relationship between what Sue said and Joe's earlier suggestion?"

"What will be the impact of this on our project's goal?"

"What did they say that was the same? What did they say that was different?"

Predicting questions – Think through things from another perspective.

"What if …?"

"What would this enable us to do?"

"How will this affect our present operation?"

"What might be a new direction for us to take?"

Beware of Reflection Stoppers

Often when people try to think together, the thinking gets stopped short by someone's remark of high emotion, criticism or unrelated comment. Learn what to ask to keep the thinking flowing when it gets bogged down.

Remember it is the "together" that is the challenge in thinking together.

Figure 7 shows three illustrations of reflection stoppers and suggestions for regenerating reflection.

Three Examples of Reflection Stoppers

Reflection Stoppers	FFID Screen *The intent for your response*	Reflective Questions *One possible response*
"Well, everyone knows ..."	Get more than one person's facts and experience	**Probe** *It is helpful to hear from several people. Somebody else, what's your experience with this? Somebody else?*
"I don't care what is said, I just don't think we can do it ..."	Get feelings and experiences out and on the table and then push the reflection to implications or a decision	**Probe, Relate, Predict** *This is an emotional issue we need to talk through. Know that all that's said will be held in confidence. What is bugging you most about this issue? Where were you surprised about what was said/not said? What do we need to do to move forward?*
"That is wrong. The X Factor Software is the only one that will work ..."	Get out everyone's facts, feelings and implications	**Probe, Clarify, Relate** *Can you help us understand your thinking? Anybody, what do you hear them saying? What is another perspective? What is different/what is the same in what we are saying?*

Figure 7

Use the examples in this chart to help you form questions that will restart reflection when a reflection stopper has brought the thinking to a close.

Develop Innovative Methods

**"Much of the energy and drive to pursue goals and engage
in essential tasks comes from the search for meaning."
– Teaching and the Human Brain[13]**

Share Approaches That Work

One of the most innovative reflective methods is deceptively simple. A
Sharing Approaches That Work (Figure 8) conversation is a good way to trigger
new thinking and learning. When people have an opportunity to share what is
working and what is not, they often make interesting discoveries:

"Other people are using some of the same approaches that I'm
discovering work well."

"I understand why that didn't work, but what we learned was valuable."

"Several of us are learning the same things that can be applied to
other projects."

"I just shared a learning I didn't realize I'd learned."

Sharing Approaches That Work

What are you working on?	What is working? And why?	What has been learned from this?	What are the implications?
Please share the details of the project. Don't assume everyone knows what is being worked on.	What successes are you having? Why do you think that is? Help people be aware of their successes and "why."	Help people articulate what they may not realize they learned from the situation. Out-of-the-box thinking can be released here.	Where else can we apply what we learned? Help people "share the recipe."

Figure 8

Use this Sharing Approaches That Work conversation format to form the questions that activate sharing and learning in many situations, such as when:
1. talking with a peer
2. building onto what is working
3. building morale
4. accelerating effectiveness
5. helping team members recognize what they learned
6. cross-fertilizing ideas with team members or other departments

The Natural Thinking Process

Tap the "way we think" – the FFID process – to bring alive any method you use. As we saw earlier, our thinking naturally flows from facts and data to experiences and feelings before we assess the importance and implications. Use this flow in other methods or communication to increase reflective participation and effectiveness.

Using FFID in Proposal Writing

Bruce, a V.P. at a large urban regional bank, has an idea to set up a drive-up teller at their urban location. As he explains his idea to the bank president, he senses an attitude of approval as the president asks Bruce to write up a proposal.

Bruce enthusiastically writes a draft proposal and sends it to the executive suite. He is stunned when it comes back with a "No." That same week Bruce is in a training class where he learns about FFID. Suddenly light bulbs go off in his head. He realizes that the proposal he wrote contained only a few implications and the final decision. In the informal conversations with the president he had talked about facts, related experiences and implications, but he had left all of that out of his written proposal.

Based on this insight, Bruce rewrites the proposal in an FFID form, covering the full flow of thinking. He is gratified when the proposal comes back with a "Yes."

Using FFID in Designing a Presentation

Julie is a newly employed salesperson for an investment company. Her assignment is to go to mid-size companies and sell funds for their retirement account. In a tough economic market it is difficult to distinguish which products are best to offer to which clients. As she makes her presentations, she *realizes that she needs to engage her clients in talking about their needs and their concerns about the market to get an idea of what is best suited for them.*

Julie discovers that framing her presentation with the FFID formula gives her an advantage in understanding the client's real needs and how to meet them.

Celebrate Accomplishments

Take opportunities to broadcast what is going on and to share learning. Celebrating marks what is important, yet we tend to do it too infrequently. Allocate time to celebrate accomplishments (actions, events, activities). Do this on a regular basis – at the end of a team meeting, as part of a celebrative meal, at a special time during the work week (late Friday afternoon) or when launching a planning retreat.

Day-to-day work keeps us all so busy that we can't keep abreast of all the things that are going on. Celebrating accomplishments highlights, recognizes and publicizes the many happenings. The intent is to refresh memories, celebrate accomplishments and learn for the future.

A "Wall of Wonder" is a fun and productive way to celebrate accomplishments. Place a chart on the wall (see Figure 9, page 114). Distribute 3x5 Post-it™ (sticky) notes to everyone. Ask each person to write on three to five notes (one idea per note) describing relevant, memorable moments that occurred in a designated time period (three months, one year, or time of the project being celebrated). These can include accomplishments, people, activities, lessons learned, relearned and so on. Everyone posts his or her sticky notes on the "Wall of Wonder" in the appropriate timeframe.

Read through all the sticky notes, or if it is a big chart ask people to "mill around" and read the notes for themselves. Ask the group for any other activities or events to add. *(facts)*

Select from the following questions to guide reflection and discuss the impact of these victories and accomplishments on the future. *(feelings and implications)*

"What item surprised you?"

"Which ones had you forgotten?"

"What did you learn about someone else?"

"Which events involved the most number of people?"

"What choices did we make?"

Wall of Wonder

(Example: Nursing Unit in Urban Hospital)			
Month 1	**Month 2**	**Month 3**	**Next 6 Months**
more positive attitudes on floor, less sarcasm	question raised: "Why do some not work nights?"	patient survey	signs of respect and regard for individuals
quieter on the unit	conversation in staff meeting about opportunities	one-on-one conversations with unit manager	more interaction with patients
people able to voice concerns in staff meeting	Brian brought cookies twice	a new assignment schedule	maintain open communication
celebrated Rosie's birthday with a cake	resentment expressed at having to take more admissions	hired one new nurse	accept admissions willingly
Brian joined the unit	rearranged furniture in family waiting area	conversation in unit meeting on "patients as a challenge"	rotating assignments

Model adapted from the Institute of Cultural Affair's "Historical Scan Method."[14]

Figure 9

"What will you take back to the job to treasure as a result of this activity?"
"How would you describe this group of people at the beginning of this?"
"How have these activities moved us in the direction we want to go?"
"What would you name this period of time we have been together?"
"In light of what has been posted and said, what does this say about the
 future?" (*decision*)
"What are the next steps for us – how does this shape what we need to do?"
"What do we intend to get accomplished in the next three months?"

Invariably, more things have been accomplished than any one person
knows or remembers. Recognizing and celebrating accomplishments is exciting
and is one factor that builds trust. We can accept the fact not everything was
perfect, and yet there is a sense of celebration when people see the big picture
of what was accomplished.

Give and Receive Feedback

"Feedback is one person giving another person objective observations about his/her behavior and subjective observations about the effects of that behavior. The purpose of feedback is to invite learning in order that an individual may achieve a desired outcome. Implicit in the invitation to learn is an invitation to change one's direction or continue one's direction."[15]

To ensure continuous learning, we help each other find out what is and is not working. We receive and give feedback all the time when we are communicating. We have no choice about giving and receiving – feedback is perceived as we smile, look neutral, frown, say something supportive, something negative. Both what we do and what we don't do is received as feedback.

To be intentional in giving feedback, decide where feedback is needed. If you think of feedback only when evaluating employees, recognize places to close the feedback loop. The feedback loop includes people at all levels who need the information, such as peers, managers, customers, suppliers, administrative help and so on. Giving feedback "up" (to managers, supervisors, higher level employees) is often the most difficult. We hesitate to give feedback "up" for fear of reprisal. Form feedback as a result of best thinking, and not a result of instinct. When you want to give feedback use this three-step process:

1. Prepare
2. Formulate your feedback
3. Make your feedback timely and appropriate

Step 1. **Prepare by collecting and analyzing the data.** Get the facts and data. Understand what happened by asking questions and actively listening to the answers.

"Why do we do it this way? How do you see it working? Can you help me understand the reason for ...?"

Step 2. **Formulate your feedback** using the following components:

– Own your feedback. Your statement should begin with "I." If it is not your thinking, don't give it, because lots of good feedback – comments that can be helpful and creative – gets twisted into gossip and therefore can have a negative effect. Talk only to the person involved.

– Be objective about the facts (what you see, hear, measure, etc.), not subjective. Make the feedback specific and data-based. *When I see/hear/measure/observe*_____.

115

– Use feelings to reflect the impact of the current situation on you. Feelings provide essential information to the person receiving the feedback as you state how the behavior impacts you/the team. *It is unhelpful/frustrating/puzzling because_____.*

– Share your perception of the impact of the present action, include what needs to continue or change. *The impact on the team is_____, and an alternative might be to_____.*

– Open up the process for thinking through together what needs to happen. Be willing to keep the conversation open. *What else might you suggest?*

Step 3. Make your feedback timely and appropriate.

– Avoid giving feedback too long after the fact, because it has less impact then.

– Give corrective feedback privately.

– Give feedback with the intent of helping the person improve and grow.

– Begin with positive feedback. Your role of scribe for the team has been helpful. Be sure to recognize the efforts and contribution made by the individual.

– Keep your feedback professional, not personal.

Reasons why managers are hesitant to give feedback include:

"We think it is none of our business."

"We don't think people will listen to us."

"We want to be polite and not hurt anybody's feelings."

"We are afraid people will take it as criticism."

"We are afraid people will try to get even if we tell what we think."

Thomas Friedman[16] comments, "There are two kinds of critics in life: those who criticize (give feedback) you because they want you to fail and those who criticize you because they want you to succeed. And people can smell the difference a mile away. If you convey to people that you really want them to succeed, they will take any criticism you dish out. If you convey that you really hold them in contempt, you can tell them that the sun is shining and they won't listen to you."

Be Facilitative from the Side

Even when you are not in charge, you can be facilitative from the side. You can play a supporting role any time as illustrated by David in the following scenario.

> *The meeting is off track. The item being discussed is not on the agenda and if it relates to what the team is working on, David doesn't see the connection. He looks around and sees at least one other person who also seems lost. The person leading the meeting seems unaware of the problem.*
>
> *To facilitate from the side, David first checks his intent – Why am I about to intervene? What is my purpose? What is the purpose of this meeting? Then he checks to see if he is the only one having trouble making the connection by saying, "It might just be me, but did we just jump off track? If not, can you help me make the connection between this and what we were talking about so I can get back on track?"*

Too often a reaction such as David's is not acted on but is simply uttered in the hallway after the meeting. "Yeah, another hour of wasted talk. It would be great if she would just keep things on track." Although everyone in the room felt the impact of time wasted, most did not feel responsible or comfortable saying something.

> *The manager has just announced some department changes during the meeting. You sense that there are some assumptions underneath the announcement that need to be aired. You look around the room and see others who look as if they, too, have questions.*
>
> *Check your intent. What is the purpose of your intervening? You decide that asking for a bigger perspective will help you and others "get on board." In a nonthreatening manner, you say, "I understand that these changes are definite. But it would help me get a bigger perspective to hear a little more about what is driving these changes. Would that be possible?"*

If such questions are not asked, many people leave with unanswered questions. Without a reason for why something is happening, they tend to make up their own reason. Made-up "whys" often come from rumors and gossip and can cause a lot of confusion.

You can ease the process for the group in a meeting whether or not you are in charge.

The more that our day-to-day interactions can be facilitative and strategic, the more learning is generated. As one manager told us, "Through using the facilitative technique of questioning, I was able to notice what information was present and what was missing. I could then draw out missing information and fill in the gaps. I could use these concepts to guide meetings from the side – without seeming bossy and taking over."

Reflection releases creative, innovative thinking. Personally commit to raise reflective questions at every possible opportunity to examine values, encourage the group and release creative thinking. Listen for the reflection generated from the dialogue you initiate. Listen for the knowledge and learning created from the collective data. Such reflection often takes on a life of its own and can go in unexpected and innovative directions.

One manager shared her experiences, "I've used these facilitative concepts very effectively at work and also in parent-teacher meetings, Sunday school classes, and especially with my three teenagers and my husband. I've also taught our kids how to use these techniques and it seems to have helped their confidence/attitudes/relationships/even their grades … and that's miraculous to me!"

Summary

You can't make people think together. People have to decide for themselves that thinking together is needed; they have to believe it will make a difference. In a time when full engagement of the workforce is crucial, reflection is the number one tool. As we talk with each other, new perspectives and knowledge turn into learning opportunities.

Tap into the natural thinking process when asking questions and release individual "I" thinking and team "WE" thinking. As we reflect together, we convert data and information into knowledge and wisdom. Experience the magic of thinking together to figure things out.

Ignite Action

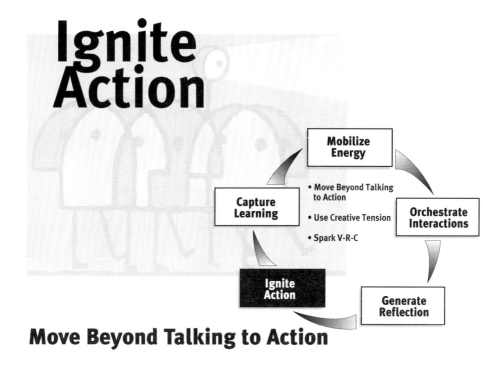

Mobilize Energy

• Move Beyond Talking to Action

• Use Creative Tension

• Spark V-R-C

Capture Learning

Orchestrate Interactions

Ignite Action

Generate Reflection

Move Beyond Talking to Action

"Knowing it ain't the same as doing it."
– Old Hoosier saying

Talking isn't doing. We have all experienced sitting in a meeting and realized that ideas were floating away like helium-filled balloons only to leave the meeting thinking,

"Another meeting with lots of good talk but little action."

"I don't understand why the same issues keep coming up over and over again. We've already addressed these."

"We started this project six weeks ago and we're still talking about it."

How do we bridge the knowing-doing gap that comes from "knowing too much and doing too little."[1] Jeffrey Pfeffer and Robert Sutton suggest that we "Make the process of doing into an opportunity to learn. Sometimes even leap into a project before you are completely sure it will work, just to learn from the experience. Or launch initiatives before every last detail is ironed out."[2]

In the old paradigm we got used to someone above us being in charge, knowing the answers and making the decisions. As a result, many employees think, "I show up, you tell me what to do, I do it, you pay me, I go home." The "I do it" stage is the problem, as either things don't get done or what is done is not what is needed. People are uncertain about learning from one another and often jealously guard information. Or there is just talk and not action. As one manager commented, "We've been processing the information for this project forever." The result is unproductive action or no action.

Make Things Happen

**"The challenge for business people is to draw new maps,
create new measures, reinvent themselves and their companies
in the context of the knowledge economy."
– Alan Webber[3]**

It is time to quit talking and start taking action. Today's challenge is to shift mindsets and behavioral skills so that everyone knows how to make action happen and takes responsibility for it.

The people involved in a given situation need to be the ones who solve the problems, which means shifting the energy flow to the group. When people broaden their perspective and work "on behalf of" each other and the task, they can take responsibility for getting things done. Ownership is energizing, awakening people to their own potential. They are empowered to make a difference using their knowledge, tools and capabilities.

Where does your organization stand in equipping people (at all levels) to think and act with a sense of ownership? Use the assessment in Figure 1 to see how your organization measures up.

After determining the score on your assessment, determine which methods and skills in this book to use to facilitatively and strategically shift the "seldoms" and "nevers" to "always" and "sometimes."

Invent the Future

It is often hard to imagine the future and identify the results you are passionate about and willing to pay the price to achieve. Think of the results you want, the ones about which you are passionate. Regularly ask the deceptively simple question, "What future results do I want to create?" Inventing the future requires a sense of ownership. A sense of ownership in turn requires learning from the past, living in the present and thinking in the future.

Learning from the past – your past as well as the experience of others teach you how to craft the future and live in the present. Select mentors. Read about them, find out what they did and did not do. Apply that knowledge to

Assessing Workers' Sense of Ownership

	Always	Often	Sometimes	Seldom	Never
1. Do you attract and keep the best people?	5	4	3	2	1
2. Do people feel empowered?	5	4	3	2	1
3. Does everyone have access to critical information?	5	4	3	2	1
4. Are people everywhere solving problems?	5	4	3	2	1
5. Is the work environment motivational?	5	4	3	2	1
6. Are people asking for training?	5	4	3	2	1
7. Are people encouraged to risk even to the point of mistakes?	5	4	3	2	1
8. Do people listen to each other?	5	4	3	2	1
9. Do people operate from the big picture?	5	4	3	2	1
10. Do people exhibit passion for what they do?	5	4	3	2	1

Scoring Key:

10-20 Your organization is not operating in a shared "ownership" model.
21-30 There is some ownership but not enough to energize the organization.
31-40 The organization is working hard toward the goal of widespread responsibility and ownership. Energy and enthusiasm are growing.
41-50 People are responsible and operating in an ownership mode.

Figure 1

your own beliefs: assess what is self-limiting and what is self-freeing.

Living in the present – creates tension with the future you are passionate about. When you feel the tension between thinking in the future and living in the present, you will take more notice of how you use time, make decisions, allocate resources, arrange space, seek training and recognize and reward effort.

Thinking in the future – is all about passion, not wishes. Inventing the future is not easy. Give yourself permission to make it up. Begin by making a list of the results you are passionate about at work, at home or on a personal level. The more you push at what you really want, the more you will wrestle with giving yourself permission to do it, and the more responsibility for creating the future will be yours.

If you work at this, you will experience more flexibility and more enthusiasm in your response to daily situations. "Yes" will come more quickly than "No." You will feel less frustrated by the present and believe more strongly each day that you can invent the future.

Check Your Own Attitude

We approach change with one of three attitudes.

Leave things as they are. "We've always done it this way" often seems the easiest, but the attitude of maintaining the status quo resists change and deflects ownership and responsibility.

Change for change sake. Sometimes enthusiasm runs ahead of methodical and/or reflective thinking. This approach can lead to chasing every good idea, and can (and usually does) boomerang. Making a change that isn't related to strategic intent is apt to create more problems than it solves.

Work in the real world. This requires a thinking, planning, reflective response and is the most reasonable choice when we are being facilitative and effective. Look reality squarely in the face – neither denying nor polishing it – asking "What is really needed?" "What is really going on?" "What is the responsible approach?" As your orientation shifts toward the future, this attitude moves you toward the important – that which will make a difference – rather than the urgent – the squeaky wheel that seems immediate.

Reflecting on what you really want to have happen, both as an individual and as a group, opens up your imagination to possibility. If you are passionate about inventing the future, you need to ask yourself every day, "What do I really want?"

Use Creative Tension

"Either you spend energy creating what you want, or you spend energy coping with what you have. Which do you prefer?"
– Anonymous

The tension between what we want (vision) and what we have (reality) is creative tension (structural tension as Robert Fritz[4] called it) and can make things happen.

Think about tension as the energy for change.

The challenge is to manage this tension between vision and reality so that we can stretch ourselves and discover what needs to be done.

Think of a personal situation when you really wanted to get something done and did it. Perhaps you completed a work project, remodeled a room, earned a degree and so on. Look at the process in Figure 2 and fill in the blanks. You will discover how this same process of thinking about what you want and then facing reality leads you to the choices you make in everyday activities.

Process for Getting Something Done

① Your situation:
A personal situation when I wanted to get something done and did it.

_____

② The length of time I planned before I decided to start _____

What triggered me to start? _____

③ My vision	④ My reality
What I wanted was ...	The reality I was faced with was ...

⑤ The choices I made were ... _____

_____

⑥ The follow-up I did was ... _____

_____

⑦ The results were ... _____

Figure 2

Steps 3, 4 and 5 enable us to use the creative tension between the present reality and our vision of the future. First, we picture the future (the vision of what we want). Second, we identify the things that need to change so that we can realize our future. And third, we choose how we will get there by strategically making a choice of where to allocate our time, energy and resources.

One participant at one of our seminars talked about running for the school board. At first she thought she was running unopposed, but on the final day for filing, three more people decided to run. In the following weeks leading up to the election, she constantly repeated to herself what she really wanted (to make a difference as a school board member) and what her current reality was (three tough opponents with name recognition). The tension between her vision and reality gave her the energy to knock on doors for six weeks. She won!

Create a Practical Vision

Facilitative Approach

Decide where you want to go. You have to make it up because if you knew the answer, you'd already be there. Begin by talking about the future and what is needed. Study the marketplace, track the competition. Create an urgency as you talk with your team about what is going on. Then constantly clarify what you want (not how to get it) and what you have (not why it got that way). Create tension between what you want and what you have to generate energy and heighten the group's focus.

Creative tension is present when vision is alive and current reality is clear. The trick is to keep the tension steady and ever forward-thinking. If you allow the tension to slacken, the hope you generated will work against you. Continually rehearsing the vision will ignite action toward that vision. Without that rehearsal, the tension pulls you back to the present.

A practical vision creates a vivid picture of the future so people are excited about what is possible.

- **Focus the practical vision as much as possible.**
   "What would we see and hear going on if our meetings were as effective as possible?" is a better question than "What do we want for our meetings?"

- **Have people stand in the future and describe what they see going on.**
    "Standing three months from now and looking back, describe what we will have done to successfully complete this project."
- **Paint as detailed and vivid a picture as possible to capture the vision.**
    When you can see it, you have a better chance of achieving it.
    Ask reflective questions like:
    "What will we be doing?"
    "What roles will we be playing?"
    "What tasks will we have completed?"
    "How will we be managing this?"
    "What will we hear people saying?"
    "What systems will be operating?"
    "How will we be relating to each other/other departments/ our customers?"
- **Help people talk about what "I will be doing" so individual passion gets tapped.**
    "Where do you see yourself in this practical vision?"
    "What do you plan to be doing?"
    "What interests you the most about this project?"
    "What role do you need to play and why?"
    "Where will your skills be best put to use? Why?"
- **Help people think outside the box.**
    Suspend questions of time, money and authorization. These questions limit thinking and are better addressed when thinking about reality and choices. Keep the images both as creative and practical as possible.

We have developed our vision when a clear, shared picture of possibility has been created. When we can see it, we have a better chance of achieving it.

Identify Current Reality

Once the vision of possibility exists, most people get excited and jump into "Here's what we need to do," bypassing the critical question of "What will stop us?" or "What is in our way?" after creating a vivid practical vision. Instead, you need to identify possible barriers or blocks. You don't work on the vision, you work on removing the blocks to the vision. Blocks are the root causes that stop the vision from becoming reality.

A barrier or block is:
- a roadblock between what exists and your vision of the future
- a challenge, not something "wrong"
- a window into the action needed
- the cause of the frustration, not just a symptom
- a clue to what is not happening, not "a lack"

Blocks may be structures, situations, procedures, routines, attitudes or policies that prevent the vision from becoming a reality. Seeing the real situation may be painful, but it is crucial to igniting action toward the vision.

When the vision is clear, it will throw a new light on the present situation and make the blocks stand out in stark relief. For example, a messy room is not a block until it is clear that the vision is a pleasant work environment, free of clutter. Similarly, a noisy, constantly interrupted work environment is not a block until it is clear that fully engaged workers are part of the vision.

Identifying blocks does not need to be a formal process. The objective is to observe and describe what is going on in the present situation as it relates to the vision. If you want a more formal method, need a way to handle a lot of data or want to involve a number of people in the process, you can use the Workshop Method, a five-step process defined later in this chapter (pages 137-141) which is designed to capture a group's thinking and move to a resolution.

Typical blocks and their location in today's workplace are apt to be those listed in Figure 3.

Look at the current reality to detect the blocks to your new vision. Include the critical question, "If this practical vision is to become our current reality, what will have to change?" Ask lots of reflective questions to find out what will stand in the way.

"What will need to change for us to reach the vision?" (Pay close attention to values, beliefs, and mindsets)

"What roadblocks will we encounter as we move toward our vision?"

"What underlying challenges do we need to address?"

When you are trying to figure out what needs to change, it is important to focus on what you see and hear. Objectivity is critical, along with the ability to keep asking the question, "Why is this still going on?"

Sometimes the conversation on "What needs to change" raises the question of "What is in/out of our control?" If this happens, encourage people to divide the list into "within our circle of control" and "within our circle of influence."

Things "within our circle of control" are those actions and events that we are empowered to decide. Things "within our circle of influence" are actions and events over which others will decide, but about which we can make suggestions. Keep in mind the things that are working now.

"What in our present situation is working with us?"

"What can we use to our advantage?"

Location of Blocks That Are Barriers to Effective Action

Locations	Descriptions
Purpose and vision	• unfocused, short-range, unclear, unsupported, past-oriented
Values	• nonoperational, undefined, conflicting, weakened
Environment	• bureaucratic, fragmented, past-oriented, neglected
Innovative methods	• minimal, underutilized, ineffective, short-range
Attitude	• cynical, passive, unenthusiastic, irresponsible
Customer issues	• unclear needs, obsolete feedback, narrow definition of the customer
Access to information	• costly, excessive, disorganized, limited, ineffective
Expectations	• confusing, overlapping, undefined, bewildering
Accountability	• misunderstood, misleading, inconsistent, unfocused

Figure 3

Lack of time, money and people are not blocks. They are symptoms of unresolved issues. Look at the systems, structures and beliefs that make these seem like barriers or blocks. Figure 4 shows the clues to the real blocks.

Clues to the Real Blocks

Obvious answer	Closer to the real block
Lack of time	Mixed priorities; too many high priorities
	Unclear of the importance
Lack of money	Missing knowledge about the cost of things
	Confusing budgeting process
	Unclear financial priorities for work
Lack of people	Limited buy-in for what is needed
	Inadequate recruiting, hiring and/or retention process

Figure 4

Listen to each other long enough to discover the real blocks and their root causes. When a block (what needs to change) has been clearly stated, it points the way to what needs to be done to remove it or work around it.

> *The managers and supervisors for an assisted living facility met for two days to articulate their practical vision and current reality. Two elements of their vision were: Provide Quality Care and Develop Effective Teamwork. They stated that the blocks to these elements of their vision included:*
> * *We don't make service a priority*
> * *The turnover of staff is high*

The statement of these blocks opens the window for these managers and supervisors to discover new ways to make service a priority and to support staff to reduce the high turnover. Once blocks are revealed, people tend to feel both overwhelmed by what needs to be done but also relieved to finally see how to deal with nagging issues and concerns. This is a good time for reflective questions to help a team take ownership of what needs to happen:

"Which of these blocks will be easiest to deal with and why?"
"Which will be the most challenging and why?"
"What do we see now that we didn't before?"
"What have we learned about our present situation?"

Choose the Future

**"Tension is the source of creativity.
It calls for and produces a response."
– Basil Sharp[5]**

Focus the choice of actions to remove blocks to the vision. Since what we have to work with is time, energy and resources, the choices we make need to focus on the use of time, energy and resources to make actions strategic rather than random.

Step 1. Brainstorm actions that will remove the blocks

The more detail, the better. Focus thinking by asking:

"What action would remove this block?"
"Why is it strategic?"
"How does it lead toward the vision?" (Detail provides specific action steps)
"What actions would remove several blocks?"
"What actions do we need to take in the next three months?"

Step 2. Develop Strategies and Actions

Decide the strategies, the broad arenas of action that will address the blocks to activate the vision. Then work with each strategy to determine the concrete actions you could see someone do (e.g., An employee energy savings plan strategy might have a van-pool action). The actions need to be doable and include what the team can do.

Skills training is often identified as a strategy, yet innovative methods, rather than basic skills, is the point of leverage in the knowledge dynamic in the organization (see page 44). When skills training is identified as a strategy, reexamine how to achieve the most leverage. Examine the idea that more knowledge may be needed by thinking through innovative methods – practical knowledge, experience wisdom or formal methods. "Do we need innovative methods to reinforce cross-interaction between teams?" (leverage points – develop innovative methods and release team spirit). "Is clarity of expectations and leadership modeling needed?" (leverage point – articulate clear expectations)? Strategic actions happen when time, energy and resources are allocated to remove blocks to the agreed-upon vision. Audit the use of time, energy and resources to remove blocks.

"How are we solving day-to-day problems?"

"What priorities are on our agenda?"

"How are resources of people and money allocated?"

"How do we use our time and space?"

"What needs to change in our communication, in our training, in the stories we tell?"

Step 3. Prioritize the Actions

Develop a timeline for detailed action. When building the timeline, consider everyone's limited amount of time, energy and resources. Clarify what to stop doing, start doing, keep doing and do differently to accomplish the plan. Success depends on how well you prioritize.

Figure 5 is a sample template for a time chart of actions. Across the top of the chart enter time periods for various actions. In the left column, write each strategy. Use sticky notes for each action step to make it easy to move the steps around in the process of prioritizing.

Work on the action steps either as a large group or in several small teams if the plan is extensive and you need more time to decide action steps. This is a "divide and conquer" strategy that works well when there is more to do in the designated time than one group can do. Additional actions often emerge from the conversation as work is done on prioritizing the strategies.

There is a tendency to put most action steps in the front end of the time period. Such enthusiasm is great but can get squashed by the reality of limited time, energy and resources. The closer the time period is to the present, the more details each action step needs to include. For deadlines that are further out, you can create a plan with fewer details, adding details as the time period gets closer.

Time Chart of Actions

	Jan.-March	April-June	July-Sept.	Oct.-Dec.
Strategy #1 **Focus on the Important**	**What:** Identify steps to start the "can dos" **Why:** spark creativity **Who:** Joe and Sue **Where:** lunch room	**What:** Communicate and implement **Why:** show seriousness **Who:** Joe and Sue **Where:** newsletter and bulletin boards		
Strategy #2 **Test the Waters**		**What:** Meet to decide areas of influence **Why:** get inside the energy **Who:** Norma and Myra **Where:** staff meetings		**What:** Give feedback to group to take next steps **Why:** celebrate team **Who:** Donna and Scott **Where:** council
Strategy #3 **Provide Cheerleading to Build the Team**			**What:** Show Ideo video in breakrooms **Why:** relief and recharge **Who:** Jill and Juanita **Where:** breakrooms	

Figure 5

Have the group look back through the initial time chart of actions. Reflect together on the prioritizing process.

"Which actions must proceed others?"

"What else is on our calendars that isn't on this chart and might impact our plan?"

"If someone new just walked in, what would they say we are trying to accomplish in the next period of time?"

Step 4. Assign the Actions

Clarify who will do what by when. Build the action plan in "real time" by considering what is already on the schedule as you add action items. Complete the time chart by clarifying the remaining W's: Why it is important to get done, Who will do which part of the job, Where it will happen. (What and When have already been decided.) Ask people to think about how each action positions them to remove the block and reach the vision. As you facilitate this conversation, keep the Dynamics Screen and the leverage points (page 44) in mind. Guide the conversation to gain the most leverage from anticipated actions.

Detailed action plans that extend beyond ninety days will most likely change. As part of the process, meet at least every quarter to assess what has changed and what you've learned. Refine the next steps as is necessary. It is important to keep remembering that we have the power to choose. The tension between what we want and what we have requires a choice.

The V-R-C facilitative process as recapped in Figure 6 helps us choose wisely. It shows the need to harness the creative tension between what needs to happen (practical vision) and what has to change (current reality) to reveal the strategic actions (critical choice) to be taken.

> **"A change in perception does not alter facts.
> It changes their meaning though – and very quickly."**
> **Peter Drucker[6]**

The V-R-C Process

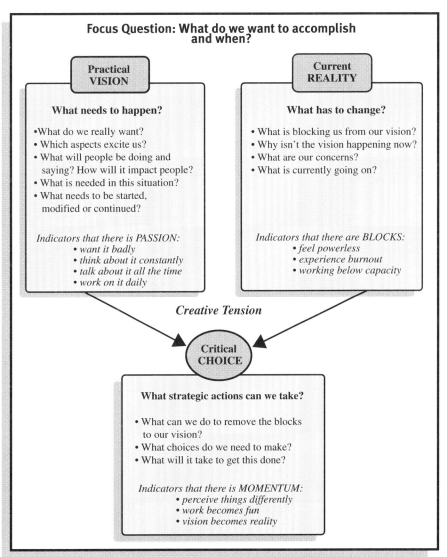

Figure 6

Spark V-R-C ...

... to Provide Direction

How-to Action

If action is not happening, some element in V-R-C (vision, reality, choice) is missing. You have already determined the vision. A good look at reality has revealed a window on how to move. So it must be direction that is missing for the action. Ask questions to figure out what to start, stop, keep doing or do differently:

"What do we need to stop doing?"

"What are we currently doing and how does it need to change?"

"How does this fit in with other priorities?"

"Do we have our time and resources allocated effectively? Why or why not?"

Listen for the real priorities that make things happen.

Listen for the real priorities that make things happen. If you do not hear any, help people verbalize them. Listen to determine which area, vision or reality requires the most attention so that tension creates the energy for choice.

When vision needs emphasis, for example, give people help in seeing possibility. Ask questions that point to the future:

"What do you want to get accomplished?"

"How will things be different in six months?"

"How will people be thinking differently?"

"How much of the vision is shared by the whole team?"

Listen for how clear the marketplace needs are. Do we have common operating values and clear roles? Listen for clarity in the specifics and, if fuzzy, help people create clarity.

Reality needs emphasis if people are excited about their vision but cannot sustain actions to make it happen. Ask:

"Where is the marketplace challenging us to change? Why?"

"What in the present situation is working against us? Why?"

"What is it that people do not want to change? Why?"

"What is the biggest struggle from your perspective? Why?"

Pay close attention to what people don't say when they are talking about why they cannot move forward. Make sure their assumptions are out in the open. For example, prompt, "Could you say a little more about your thinking on this?" "Share with us the thinking behind your statement." "Why is that important?"

> *An investment company's managers were putting together a 401(k) presentation for their clients. They usually lectured, but clients were requesting more education. The idea of being more facilitative in their presentations raised a number of questions:*
>> *"Wasn't being facilitative going to mean adding a twenty-minute activity to the presentation we already have?"*
>> *"We have our presentation down pat, so why work harder?"*
>> *"How can we deal with people who don't give the expected answers?"*
>> *"We can probably engage a client who is a high school graduate but what can we do to engage the PhDs?"*
> *The managers chose one curriculum module as a pilot to learn how to shift the style from "presentation" to "facilitative." Their intent was to help clients become better decision-makers for their 401(k) assets. A chart of the current curriculum revealed ways to spark V-R-C to provide direction and facilitate the learning process. Incorporating reflective questions would ensure engaging the clients in building their own retirement plans. This allowed clients a new sense of direction. Figure 7 (page 136) illustrates the facilitative plan they designed.*

"Action will remove the doubt that theory cannot solve."
– Tehyi Hsieh[7]

Retirement Plan Services — Investing with a Purpose

Opening	Achieve Your Purpose with the Three Principles					Closing
	Vision	Reality	Principle #1: Let Your $$ Work for You Compound Interest	Principle #2: Get Ahead of Inflation Know Your Risk (Strategic Choices)	Principle #3: Find Your Mix Diversify (Strategic Choices)	
Outcome for the presentation: Participants continue (or start) to fully utilize their 401(k) plan. *Intent: Know – the power of compound interest, two types of risk, diversify. Experience – This is about ME. Driven by my hopes & dreams, sobered by reality, moved to take action.*	• Vision for your retirement life style	• What it will take	• The result of compound interest	• Inflation example	• Why diversify	*Reflection: Take a minute and thumb through notes. They write in their book. Ask: What's one key point of this presentation? What do these tell us to do? Listen for opportunities to teach.*
• Hello	*Interaction: Worksheet*	1. Each person finds his/her own numbers	*Reflection: What strikes you?*	*Reflection: Their illustrations of this concept, then our illustrations*	• The 401(k) options in your plan (use as a way to review stocks, bonds, MM)	• Enroll in automatic investment plan
• Lots of reasons for us to invest – retirement is our focus		*Interaction: Locate your #s and write them down*	• Lesson: Pay yourself first		*Reflection: Their experience with stocks, bonds, MM*	• Take advantage of dollar cost averaging
• We will approach this by looking at:		2. Sources for retirement $$	*Interaction: Chart to figure out what you need*	• Know your risk: two types	*Interaction: Assessment to find your MI.*	• Invest for the long term
1. Vision for your retirement life style		*Reflection: Who is ready to try out for "Millionaire"?*	*Interaction: Ask participants to identify next steps*		*Reflection: What did you learn/discover? (This reflection lets participants define the lesson of this section.)*	• Be patient
2. What it will take ... find your #s	*Transition: Any time you look at your hopes and dreams, it is important to check out reality also.*	*Transition: On TV's "Want to Be a Millionaire," there is only one winner. With the 401(k) everyone wins. Let's look at the those principles now.*	*Transition: Good news/bad news*	*Transition: Lesson: Let both types of risk help you find your MIX.*	• Ask for Action	*Closing: Tell vision-reality-choice story. "Keep your Retirement Vision in Focus."*
3. The Three Principles					*Transition: Let's pull this all together by reviewing the key points.*	

Figure 7

Spark V-R-C ...

... to Problem Solve

V-R-C can be used to guide your problem-solving efforts. For example, a consensus Workshop Method can be used with a group to discover the vision, determine reality and/or decide choices.

The consensus Workshop Method captures people's ideas and moves a group toward a resolution of the group's focus question. The method is highly interactive, going beyond individual ideas to create new insights and generate ownership for the intended result. The consensus Workshop Method converts a brainstorm list into action, then builds on the results, creating action projects with tangible accomplishments, milestones, completion dates and delegated responsibilities. Jon Jenkins, in *The International Facilitator's Companion*, says, "The Workshop Method enables people to see new relationships. It helps a group work cooperatively. It is intended to enable a group to build a model and come to a decision. It is a tool for creating a polylogue (a many-sided discussion)."[8]

The consensus Workshop Method follows the sequence shown in Figure 8.

The Workshop Method

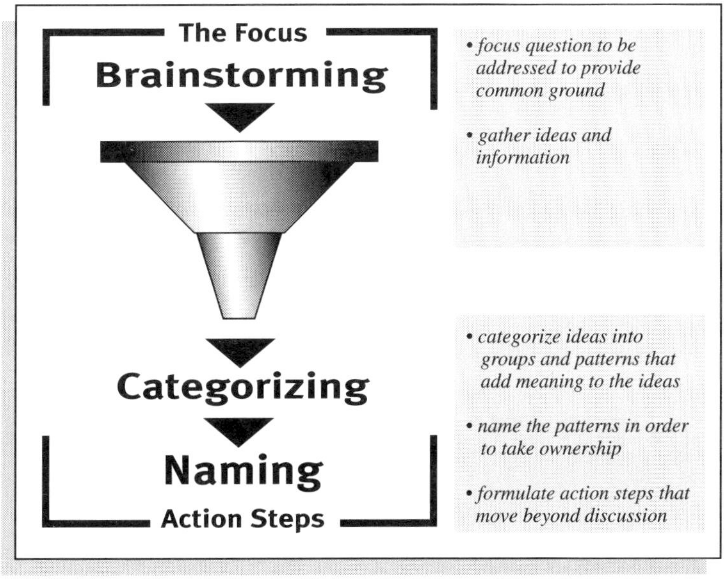

- The Focus
- **Brainstorming**
  - *focus question to be addressed to provide common ground*
  - *gather ideas and information*
- **Categorizing**
  - *categorize ideas into groups and patterns that add meaning to the ideas*
- **Naming**
  - *name the patterns in order to take ownership*
- Action Steps
  - *formulate action steps that move beyond discussion*

Figure 8

#1. Create a focus question

Usually the manager or person facilitating the discussion/meeting creates the focus question in advance. Prior to the workshop, consult with several of the people involved to verify that the focus question is on target. Then, before the workshop, write out the focus question. Include the topic and time frame. For example, "How can we reduce the operating budget by 10 percent without a loss of customer satisfaction within the next two years?"

At the beginning of the workshop read the focus question, and, if possible, post it on the wall for everyone to see during the workshop. Verify that all participants are in agreement on the focus question before moving forward. "Is this what we need to be focusing on?" "Are we all clear? Is there anything you do not understand about this question?"

#2. Brainstorm ideas

Brainstorming releases people's insights and creativity. Ask participants to put ideas down on paper so they can share them with their working group. If it is a large group, work in smaller groups to pull together the best ideas.

1. Ask individuals to write down five or six ideas (vision elements, issues, actions – depending on the intent of the workshop) that would address the focus question. Encourage them to write whatever they are thinking without self-censoring (e.g., "This is a good idea, but too costly, time-consuming for me to add.")
2. Have them star their two best ideas.
3. In small groups of three to five people, have participants:
   - Share all starred ideas
   - Eliminate duplications
   - Quickly review the rest of the ideas and pick out any other important ones
4. Share ideas as a whole group. Put selected ideas on the wall (sticky notes or list on a white board) in a three- to five-word summary. If you need to put more detail, capture it on a note pad or the reverse side of the sticky note. Clarify but don't critique when sharing brainstorming ideas. Be sure that each participant has an opportunity to share at least one idea (round robin), then let the ideas fly. Remember to write down the exact words a person says when recording on the flip chart.

#3. Categorize ideas into patterns that give meaning

1. Organize the ideas by grouping them into categories of shared intentions. Listen for how the information leads to new insights as it is shared.

   Ask people to put similar ideas together. If listing on a white board, you can use various symbols (triangle, square, star, etc.) to code similar ideas. Choose a different symbol for each category. Decide the symbol for each idea by asking, "Is this like … (a previous idea with a circle, square, etc.)?" If ideas are on sticky notes, group them by similar ideas in columns on a white board (or wall). Ask questions that help people see patterns and/or categories:

   "Which ideas have similar intentions?"
   "What is the common thread tying these ideas together?"
   "Does this make sense – any other perspectives?"
   "Could you say a bit more about why you see those two are the same?"

   As you categorize ideas have a screen in mind (e.g., the Dynamics Screen: economic-political-cultural or markets-purpose-involvement).

2. When working with columns on the white board, put a temporary name on the categories, A, B, C, and so on, as they begin to form. Don't force an idea into a category. As data are put up, more categories may emerge.

3. Ask teams to look at the remaining ideas and determine if they go in one of the categories or if they belong to a new category. Place ideas in the appropriate category. Continue this process until all the ideas have been categorized. Read through the new additions. Check for clarity.

Thinkabouts in Categorizing

Thinkabout

- Typically, 80 percent of the categories will emerge in the first half of the brainstorm data.
- Be careful that categories don't form too quickly. When there are a lot of data, there is a tendency to overprocess and not create enough categories. Usually there will be four to seven categories.
- Pace the categorizing process. Moving too slowly will not keep people engaged. Moving too fast might lose some people.
- When a group struggles to decide where the data go, it is helpful to ask the person who wrote it, "Tell us more about what you meant by …"

- Don't let one or two people determine categories as this diminishes group ownership. Keep tuned to the group, not the sticky notes on the wall. Continue to ask questions: "Does this make sense? Any other perspectives? Let's move this there for now and move it again later if needed – ok?" If needed, re-categorize to capture the uniqueness that might have been missed.

4. Name the categories

Giving a name to something gives it meaning. The name of a category allows the group to see its implications. Coming up with a name is three-fourths of the solution. Several ideas might move to another category during this step.

To guide the group's thinking about assigning names, ask questions that:
1. Determine the topic represented by the category – communication, training, leadership, purpose, etc.
2. When discovering the root of a problem, add a difficulty word to the topic by asking, "What is the difficulty here, what do we have now in (topic)?" (e.g., unpredictable communication channels, limited training opportunities, controlling leadership, etc.).
3. When determining an action, add an action word to the topic by asking, "What do these ideas tell us needs to happen with (topic)?" (e.g., create regular communication updates, design new orientation training, clearly define the purpose, etc.).

Encourage people to create a sound bite that captures the information in a given category. The more memorable and descriptive the name is, the more vivid and memorable the information. Do one together. Then, if just a few people are doing all the talking, assign small teams to work on naming the categories. Write the category name so it stands out (use a different-color sticky note, a different-color marker, or put a box around the name, etc.).

When a group bogged down in trying to name the categories, finally, one participant asked the facilitator, "You know more about this than we do. Why don't you just name the categories?" The facilitator's response revealed the purpose of the naming process when he said, "You are the ones who have to save this company, not me. Therefore, the names need to be your decision."

#5. Determine next steps to move beyond discussion to action

This step turns "lots of paper around the room" into "so what does this tell us to do?"

1. Read through the category names. Then ask, "Does this capture our thinking about (the focus of this workshop) – why or why not?"
2. Remind people of the vision (as in V-R-C), then ask, "What needs to happen next to move these ideas to action?" It is not always necessary to create new "to do" lists. Look at what could be done differently – the weekly meeting can be refocused, the conversations in the hallway can take on a new intent, the project team can be redirected and so on. When thinking gets "locked up," break it loose by creating multiple scenarios, "what if we did …" scenes.

Close the workshop with reflection, for example:

"What is one thing we did here? Somebody else?"
  (get many responses)
"What was easy about what we did?"
"Where did we struggle?"
"What difference will this make?"
"What have we said we need to do next?"

See Brian Stanfield, *The Workshop Book, From Individual Creativity to Group Action,* for more on the Workshop Method.[9]

Spark V-R-C ...

... to Motivate

Passion is the fuel that keeps the internal motivation burning.

Tapping into people's passion requires aligning passions with practical vision. Figure 9 (page 142) is a graphic of the research in *If It Ain't Broke, Break It.*[10] As illustrated, when people have a passion of seven or higher for a project (on a scale of ten, with ten being high), the project is almost always successful. Passion of less than seven means the project will probably not succeed.

Align Passion with Moving Toward Practical Vision

With **Passion** for a project of 7 or above *(on a scale of 1-10)*, we get it done most of the time.		
	Task that needs to be done.	**Task that does not need to be done.**
Passion is greater than 7	Give the person support.	**Redirect the person's passion by emphasizing the practical vision.**
Passion is less than 7	**Help the person say "Yes" to the practical vision.**	Learn to say NO.

Figure 9

Passion is revealed when people are:
- willing to make things happen
- taking responsibility
- choosing to do what is needed
- defining their role relative to the vision
- using their imagination to figure out what hasn't been created yet

Listen for the level of passion:

"How much are people talking about their vision?"

"How many questions are people asking to discover more details and clarify challenges?"

"What are people saying to get others involved?"

"What are people excited about creating?"

"Why is this important for our future?"

When you are thinking facilitatively, you:

… uncover passion

- Watch for where people use their creativity or choose to do whatever is needed.
- Listen to what people are excited about or what they are asking questions about.

... support passion
- When the passion bolsters what needs to get done, support it. Do the things you would want others to do for you.
- When the passion does not support what needs to get done, redirect it.

... redirect passion
- Build a bigger picture for what needs to happen.
- Help people understand WHY this is more important than what they are already doing.

... create passion
- Include others in creating the plan.
- Remind people WHY what is being done is important.

Look through the following list. Check out which things indicate that passion levels are low:

working below capacity	being defensive
blowing smoke	feeling trapped
playing political games	experiencing burn-out
fearing the unknown	experiencing powerlessness
operating with a "no" mentality	pointing blame
letting routines get you in a rut	trying to stay out of trouble
whining about the way it is	

Reflective Learning

Vision and possibility need more emphasis to motivate and reignite passion.

Spark V-R-C ...

... to Operate Strategically

"Would you tell me, please, which way I ought to go from here?"
"That depends a good deal on where you want to get."
"I don't much care where."
"Then it doesn't matter which way you go."
– Lewis Carroll[11]

Sometimes we sound like Alice in Wonderland, not sure which way we want to go. To be strategic means to artfully and knowingly think through what it takes to achieve the preferred goal, concentrate on both the big picture and the details and to make it happen.

> *Lance Armstrong and his team in the Tour de France are constantly thinking through all the factors that might influence what happens: the climate, others' riding styles, what has occurred already, what is on the road ahead, when it is strategic to make a move, what was learned from the last Tour, and so on.*

Thinking and acting strategically allows a team to recognize and take advantage of opportunities, to figure out what is needed and decide what to do.

Thinking strategically helps the team to imagine how a situation can evolve. It allows the team to deal with the actual blocks to the vision, not just the symptoms.

Employ one or more of the five strategic modes below to ensure effectiveness in implementing actions.

1. **Intensive strategy** – the use of maximum power, energy and effort to demonstrate what can be done.
2. **Extensive strategy** – a wide move to explore strengths and weaknesses.
3. **Symbolic strategy** – a declaration of victory before the action.
4. **Probe strategy** – a fast, often high-risk move to try out an idea.
5. **Flanking strategy** – a defensive move to protect against surprise.

Figure 10 further defines how to use each of the five strategic modes by stating the objective of each strategic mode, the number of people to involve in each and the amount of energy that is needed.

Meet at least quarterly to measure progress. The vision or blocks to the vision may need to be updated, and strategies may need refreshing. Build in accountability for implementation – who does what, by when, where and why. When you agree to check in with each other regularly, you can monitor how well the strategy is working and evaluate the overall impact, allowing for mid-course adjustments (more typical than not in times of constant change).

Five Strategic Modes

Strategic Mode	Objective	Involvement Required	Energy Needed	Key Action – an Example
1. Intensive Strategy (a primary strategy)	To demonstrate that something can be done.	Assign a small number: the best people.	Stay focused but realize this uses the most time and effort of the five modes.	*A small team is assigned to create the initial physical layout for the new office.*
2. Extensive Strategy (a primary strategy)	To inform many people who need to know what is going on.	Communicate with all the people involved: get more people in the loop.	Create the big picture for a broad base of people.	*Everyone on the commission receives notification of a possible policy change.*
3. Symbolic Strategy (a primary strategy)	To create unity and spirit.	Focus on creating an atmosphere that supports what is needed. Involvement varies.	Create the symbols that reinforce purpose. Spend time and energy as needed.	*Stories of "who we are helping" are displayed to remind people of why we work here.*
4. Probe Strategy (an exploring strategy)	To test an idea or learn as much as possible about something.	Limit involvement to those who have a passion for the effort.	Choose a focused effort rather than a commitment of lots of people and time. Create evaluation criteria.	*The bank teller supervisor PILOTED the use of the new manual transaction machine.*
5. Flanking Strategy (a guarding strategy)	To protect or support information or a project as needed.	Keep close communication: involvement level varies.	Anticipate what will happen. Use a low emphasis.	*Area offices are notified of upcoming changes that might impact them.*

Figure 10

Spark V-R-C ...

... to Position People to Take Action

Igniting action is triggered with V-R-C (vision-reality-choice). Implementing action often requires positioning people, the situation, the team and the organization for what needs to be done. Let's look at how using ALPS: Awareness, Learning, Piloting and Sharing can help position people for effective action. Incorporate ALPS (see Figure 11, page 146) into your daily interactions to ensure an intentional journey toward responsible action.

ALPS

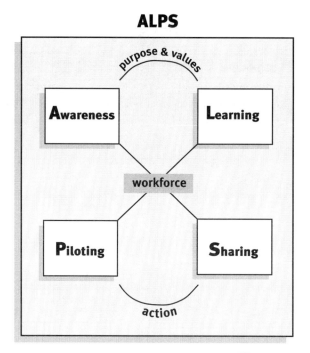

Figure 11

A – Create Awareness so people wake up to new possibilities and take responsibility. Build images of the bigger "why" – why this task, why now and why us. Create stories about the purpose of any new plan and the team's role in creating and implementing it.

Remind and challenge people to be aware of opportunities to take responsibility. This awareness is created through the way time, space and relationships are used.

You need to create more awareness when you hear:
"Now, why are we doing this?"
"But how can we possibly …?"
And see:
- Individuals not assuming responsibility
- Little understanding of consequences
To create awareness:
1. Set expectations that "stretch" responsibility. Tell people why you think

they can reach new levels of performance, initiative, leadership, responsibility and so on.

2. Hold people accountable for new expectations.
3. Praise accomplishments, and when "powerless" language creeps into the conversation help clarify goals and explore alternatives. Offer to "think together" about challenges, asking such questions as, "What responsibility do you have? What else could be done?"
4. Remind people of the purpose, the task, the vision. Display images (posters, banners, charts, etc.) of these in the work area.
5. Ask, "What do you think needs to happen?" when you are asked, "What do I need to do?"

L – Generate Learning as the task progresses so everyone has increased knowledge and capabilities. Use conversations on the task as ways to save time, energy and resources. Get to know team members, their strengths and interests. Demonstrate listening and caring by paying attention to what people are saying and listening with a "third ear" so people experience being heard. Learn from each other.

You need to generate learning when you hear:
"We keep making the same mistakes."
"If we could spend a little time getting up to speed …"
And see:
• The obvious not getting done
• Activity going on that is unrelated to the plan
The following four suggestions help generate learning.

1. Set up mentoring relationships.
2. Share relevant articles and information (include customers' and competitors' information) and reflect together on what you are reading and what it means for the daily work.
3. Ask individuals to identify areas of learning they feel would help them meet expectations. When people return from a workshop or class, ask "What did you learn? How can we apply that?"
4. Help people reflect on how much they do know. "I understand you have been working on the registration process. What are some of the activities you have been involved with? Where are you having success and why?

Where are you running into challenges and why? What are you learning? Where else can you/we apply what you are learning?" Create a climate that helps people think like this about everything they do.

P – Encourage Pilot projects. Innovate and experiment – test some things out as the work progresses. Build in tolerance for trial and error to encourage team members to learn from experimenting, and show support for people who try out new ideas. Enable people to venture beyond their comfort zone and take risks. Continue listening and observing, noting areas of growth so you can challenge them in new ways. Piloting ideas is one of the best ways to encourage calculated risk-taking and to build a learning environment in which empowerment thrives.

You need to encourage pilot projects when you hear:
"We didn't get it right the first time."
"We need something tried in a safe environment."
And see:
- A few people eager to try something new
- People locked in debate about what will work or not
The following four ideas help encourage pilot projects.
1. Encourage people to pursue their passions. Set agreed-upon expectations and let them run with it.
2. Let people try out new areas of assignment in the context of a pilot so that a learning environment is created.
   "Try this out. Be mindful of what you are learning about what works and what doesn't work. Then, let's talk about what adjustments need to be made so the next attempt is even better."
3. The next time you hear, "I can't" or "They won't let us," suggest a pilot project, if appropriate. Ask, "What can we try and learn from?"
4. Foster a "quick test" environment. For example, when debate starts about what "that other department can do," stop the debate and test it out. Pick up the phone and ask the necessary questions.

S – Practice Sharing so people are continually learning from each other. Shape communications for task-oriented sharing by building sharing and learning into every meeting. Ask questions that will enable thinking together.

Practice sharing when you hear:

"We keep reinventing the wheel."

"We don't really know what they are doing."

The same questions keep coming up on different teams.

And see:

- An "us" and "them" attitude
- Ideas caught in silos

Six ways to practice sharing include:

1. Discover how to use what is working in other situations.
2. Involve people in discussions that affect their work area.
3. Encourage cross-functional workgroups.
4. Put people together who have not worked together before.
5. Help people see the power in sharing information across boundaries by sharing information with those who need it (e.g., get customer feedback to the people that are directly responsible for providing customer service).
6. Create an empowering atmosphere by asking:

    "Where else can we apply what we are learning in this situation?"

    "Why is this so important? What difference will this make? Can you say more to help us understand your thinking?"

Check for Comprehensiveness

ALPS can help you think through the process of positioning people to take action. Because you want action to be comprehensive, check how you can use the nine dynamics (Markets, Resources, Operations, Identity, Knowledge, Style, Involvement, Controls and Decision-Making) to screen your action steps. For example:

Situation	The new team assistant, Robin, had transferred from another organization that stifled responsibility.
Vision	You want Robin to take initiative and fully utilize her talents.
Reality	She doesn't seem confident to pick up tasks and make things happen even though she is skilled to do so.
Choice	Help Robin see herself as an equal member of your team and gain confidence in her ability to give input and take initiative.

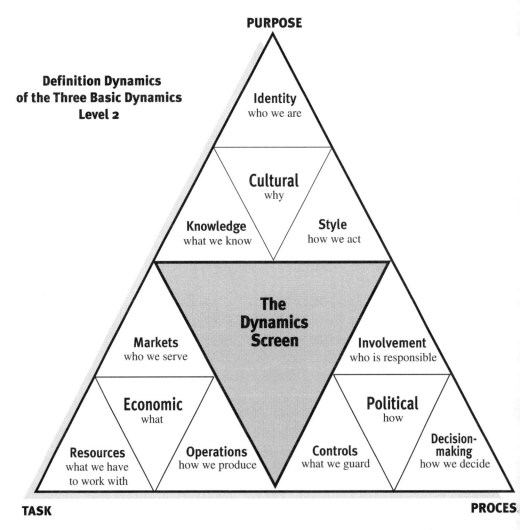

**Definition Dynamics
of the Three Basic Dynamics
Level 2**

PURPOSE

Identity
who we are

Cultural
why

Knowledge
what we know

Style
how we act

The
Dynamics
Screen

Markets
who we serve

Involvement
who is responsible

Economic
what

Political
how

Resources
what we have
to work with

Operations
how we produce

Controls
what we guard

Decision-
making
how we decide

TASK

PROCES

Figure 12

The following action steps may help Robin see herself as an equal member of the team.

Awareness
- Define her tasks and broaden responsibility
- Clarify her expectations
- Ask for her suggestions and use them so Robin sees herself as a valued team member

Learning
- Watch for aptitude
- Encourage desk-top publishing interest, supporting Robin in attending classes
- Suggest and help with new roles
- Send Robin to an investment class to learn more about our business

Pilots
- Give Robin smaller new tasks to develop her confidence
- Use some of Robin's ideas

Sharing
- Ask Robin for her input where appropriate
- Include Robin in team reflections on the week
- Urge Robin to share what she is learning

Now let us use the Dynamics Screen (Figure 12) to check the comprehensiveness of our actions with Robin.

1. Do we have action steps about the Markets (products & services, customer needs, delivery strategies) Dynamic?

    We need an action step here – Robin needs to be made aware of our customers and their needs so she can be as effective as possible. We did address sending her to an investment class.

2. Do we have action steps about the Resources (basic assets, technical capability, needed skills) Dynamic?

    We need to add an action step – help Robin understand she can let us know if she needs additional resources. She'll need to be made aware of any resource restrictions.

3. Do we have action steps about the Operations (core processes, operating systems, specialized abilities) Dynamic?

    We addressed this – Robin was made familiar with our current processes and asked for her suggestions on improving them. We also watched for new abilities.

4. Did we include or need action steps about the Identity (unique benefits, common purpose, work environment) Dynamic?

    We covered this – we helped Robin understand the purpose of tasks and broadened her responsibility. She knows how the work environment contributes to her workday.

5. Did we include or need action steps about the Knowledge (fundamental expertise, shared values, innovative methods) Dynamic?

    We covered this – we're watching Robin for aptitudes. We are encouraging desk-top publishing and sent her to an investment class.

6. Did we include or need action steps about the Style (individual roles, team spirit, flexible configurations) Dynamic?

    We covered this – Robin is included in the team's reflections, she has already suggested and helped with new roles. We've urged her to share what she is learning.

7. Did we include or need action steps about the Involvement (appropriate compensation, significant engagement, increased responsibility) Dynamic?

    This received a big emphasis – we asked for suggestions and input, and used some of Robin's ideas. Robin is included in the team's weekly reflections. We've given Robin some smaller new tasks.

8. Did we include or need action steps about the Controls (fiscal guidelines, legal requirements, monitoring structures) Dynamic?

    We might want to add to our action steps – clarify with Robin our performance measurement system.

9. Did we include or need action steps about the Decision-Making (appropriate consensus, clear expectations, regular accountability) Dynamic?

    We covered this – we have clarified expectations with Robin.

Sustain Momentum

Systems naturally fight to return to the way they were.

Usually there is enthusiasm and energy when a project is launched or a plan is initiated, but often momentum slows as barriers and obstacles begin to confront us. An intentional push is needed to sustain momentum. You can sustain forward momentum by the way you:

- Keep the practical vision in front of everybody all the time. A quick, visible victory sustains enthusiasm while work is in progress on longer-term actions.
- Tackle action in small chunks. Concentrate on manageable tasks so as not to overwhelm people.
- Use a live demonstration of one (or more) action(s). A pilot can test what will happen before you are caught up in debate and theory. Involve those who will implement the action in designing the pilot. Planning action steps for somebody else to carry out is a recipe for no action. Pilots create immediate visibility. Start one.
  - Try something out rather than write a proposal.
  - Create a small demonstration instead of a new committee.
  - Explore a new possibility with a few people.
  - Help a small group try out their new idea.
  - Ask volunteers to try out a new process, resource or service.
- Chart movement and create a picture of progress.
- Learn from each other. Use every opportunity as a learning experience. You can learn as much from failures as from successes. Try out the following team conversation.
  "We have been working to remove blocks to our vision for three weeks now. Let's reflect on what is working and what is not. Then we can decide what is needed next."
  - "As we go around the table, please share one successful action you have seen us take to remove the blocks." (*factual input to start with*)
  - "Why do you think the action you mentioned worked well?" (*individual experiences of success*)
  - "What is an action that you have been involved with that hasn't worked as you planned?" (*individual experiences of challenges*)
  - "Why do you think this was unsuccessful?" (*individual experiences of challenges*)
  - "What are we learning about what works and what doesn't?" (*interpreting what is being discovered*)
  - "What areas do we need to work on?" (*implications for the future*)
  - "Given what we have learned, what is needed next?" (*decisions that will sustain momentum*)

- Celebrate successes to communicate what is important. Celebrations and rewards do not need to be extravagant. The most important thing is that they be sincere and intentional.
- Remaneuver and adapt. In times of constant change, keep actions relevant. Build in time for remaneuvering sessions to refresh the vision, identify new blocks and think through the next strategic actions needed. Do this quarterly if you have built a vision for a whole year. If your vision is shorter term, do this step more frequently.

If forward momentum seems stalled, use a reflective conversation to discover why.

"We have been working on this project and we still seem to be blocked. Would you be willing to review our thinking again?" (*context*)

"What was one thing that we originally wanted out of this effort?" (*more responses will ignite passion for getting things done*)

"When we compared what we wanted with what we had, what needed to change?" (*try to capture everything that needs to be said*)

"When we look at all we have accomplished, which changes have been most important and how do we know?" (*be patient here and don't rush. Let people think. Some silence is OK. Go visual*)

If all the desired changes have not been made, ask, "What is keeping this change from happening?" If all the changes have been made, ask, "What blocks are still between us and our vision?"

Reach Consensus So You Are Taking Action Together

Often we want people to feel good about being "frontline decision-makers," so decisions are reached without challenging people's opinions. Not surprisingly, implementation fails because there was no commitment to make it happen. A shallow consensus produces lots of talk, little action and a bad name for the process of consensus decision-making.

Consensus does not mean that everyone agrees with the decision. In real life with real groups of people struggling with real issues, total agreement often takes too long. Consensus means that everyone has participated in, understands, and is committed to supporting a decision. It requires genuine dialogue about the issues involved and depends on discovering common ground. Consensus requires a realistic acceptance of what can be achieved in the time available and with the people involved.

Consensus is both a process and a way of thinking. Consensus thinking gets people to move together. As such, it relies on cooperation, not competition. It depends on individuals, teams and departments working for the common good of the organization

**How do you know you have a consensus? Look for action!
If there is no action, there is no consensus.**

Consensus is all about getting people moving together, not just 51 percent of them.

When a situation requires group thinking and taking action together to solve a problem, you need a consensus process. Figure 13 defines what consensus is and is not.

Don't be afraid to call for a consensus. Ask for someone to state the

Defining Consensus

Consensus is ...	Consensus is not ...

• building a new agreement
• thinking together over
  the issues
• a way to get people involved
• demonstrating commitment
• a breakthrough on how
  to do business better
• moving forward together
	• everyone agreeing with me
	• debating and negotiating
	  the issues
	• showing off for the boss
	• theorizing and philosophizing
	• talking about others and what
	  they need to do
	• the perfect decision

Figure 13

consensus. The key is to state what the team is saying, not what the individual wants to say. Call for consensus by asking, *"On behalf of us all, will someone say what you believe to be the consensus?"*

Write out the consensus. Clarify doubts and concerns. Nobody holds a veto. If someone strongly disagrees, ask for an alternative. Keep pinpointing where there is consensus. Remember people are charged to speak on behalf of the team. You cannot ask too many times ...

"Is this what we are saying we need to do?"

"Will someone state what they hear our consensus to be on this point?"

It is fine to postpone a decision if no viable consensus is ready. Encourage active participation through the use of:

- probing questions that help get all the facts and feelings on the table
- paraphrasing so people have a chance to hear the insight again with different words
- reflecting on others' concerns
- summarizing the key points

Communicate the Decision

Communicating a decision is often as important as the decision itself. Once you reach consensus, make sure that someone contacts those who need to know about the decision. Decide on the best method for transmitting this decision – a one-on-one conversation, a phone call, an email, an announcement in the newsletter. Review the information for clarity, accuracy and/or for legal/communication issues prior to making a "public" announcement. Consider the need and plans for ongoing communication within the group as well as with the larger audience.

Summary

The vision is a picture of the future, whereas the present is an audit of the now. The key is to build creative tension between the two so we face a choice and can move to action.

Learn how to effectively work with people to achieve organizational tasks by heightening the creative tension between vision and reality. Chart the direction, benchmark results, position for commitment and sustain momentum. Develop a strong belief in the ability to get action to happen together and position people to assume responsibility.

"Failure is never so frightening as regret."
– The movie: *The Dish*[12]

Capture Learning

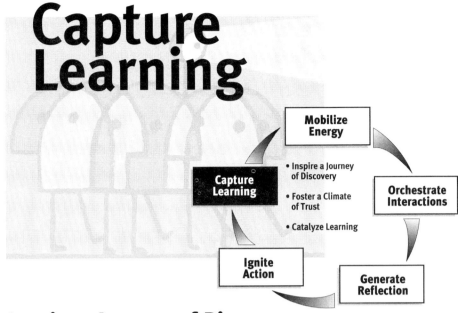

- Inspire a Journey of Discovery
- Foster a Climate of Trust
- Catalyze Learning

Mobilize Energy

Orchestrate Interactions

Generate Reflection

Ignite Action

Capture Learning

Inspire a Journey of Discovery

Share the Recipe

People used to stay with one organization their entire working life, working hard to rise to a better position. Now people are apt to change employers as many as five to seven times during their working life, voluntarily or involuntarily. How do organizations keep the best people? How can being facilitative help us share the recipe and retain the knowledge?

Peter Senge[1] defines a learning organization as "an organization that is continually expanding its capacity to create its future." A learning organization fosters team learning, genuinely encourages sharing of ideas, systems thinking and shared visioning.

It is a journey of discovery when people share what they learn; when they have time and place for reflection. Shared energy and a sense of belonging characterize the organization. Knowledge is considered capital, and policies reflect an understanding of the community environment. Further, within such an environment, teams are created and eliminated as needed. Similarly, products and services change to meet the needs of both internal and external customers.

Many organizations are involved in "learning efforts." However, this does not necessarily mean that they are learning organizations. Their efforts may be quality improvement, reengineering, downsizing, mergers, an automation program, team building, ISO 900, or becoming a learning organization. Such efforts are often perceived as "top management's thing" and do not involve everyone. In some cases the effort becomes an independent program, not owned by the participants at all. In fact, sometimes the very opposite of involving people is true: new ideas focus on increased control over people.

In learning organizations, on the other hand, everyone is encouraged to think (i.e., contribute ideas) as well as to act. This added value speeds up response time and increases flexibility by tapping creativity and involvement. No wonder that start-ups or small companies that involve everyone in both thinking about and doing the work often upstage traditional organizations.

Becoming a learning organization requires changing everyone's mindset, which, in turn, takes learning, unlearning and relearning.

As a result of this process, leadership develops at every level in a learning organization and mission and vision anchor day-to-day operations with core values.

The Industrial Revolution focused on bigger and better – maximizing profits. Today there is a shift in our understanding of what makes greatness in the journey of discovery, as reflected in such questions as, "What do we stand for?" "What are our enduring values?" "Who are we really?" In *Built to Last*, Prosser and Collins show that the truly exemplary companies (visionary companies) understand that the bottom line includes core values and compelling purpose. "David Packard and Bill Hewlett didn't 'plan' the HP Way or HP's 'WHY of business'; they simply held deep convictions about the way a business *should* be built and took tangible steps to articulate and disseminate these convictions so they could be preserved and acted upon."[2]

Work Wiser

To work wiser we need to cultivate the ability to think, talk and take action together.

Gary talked about his team's "every other Friday meeting." After every meeting team members moaned that what was accomplished in the meeting could have been done in the last five minutes. Gary finally got tired of listening to the complaints, and asked his boss after one meeting, "What three things does this group need in order to function differently in their meetings than they do now?" His boss' answer amazed Gary. "They need to think together. They need to plan and learn how to work together. It would be a miracle if they could simply talk one at a time."

The ability to reflect – to "think things through together" – is a resource we have scarcely begun to tap in most organizations. In our economy we have to be able to engage the hearts and minds of everyone. We cannot afford anyone opting out, or devote precious resources and manpower to look over someone's shoulder to see that a job gets done. Employees must be able to serve their customers (both internal and external) with responsiveness and flexibility.

"The illiterate of the 21st century will not be those who cannot read and write, but those who cannot learn, unlearn and relearn," says Alvin Toffler.[3] Working wiser can offer a new measure of workplace stability and job security.

The space shuttle Challenger disaster in 1986 is one example of missed learning opportunities. The program existed in an environment that prohibited complaining about issues, such as the lack of an escape mechanism for astronauts to get out when things got bad. The restrictive culture also stopped the engineers from raising questions that would have prevented the launch of a rocket with a faulty O-ring. Thinking, talking and acting together was not a part of that culture.[4]

Often thinking together is not focused and is not reflective, resulting in the many things that can go wrong in human thinking. When we don't pay attention, we "tend to think by default in ways that are hasty, narrow, fuzzy and sprawling."[5] Let's look at each of these individually: (a) Hasty thinking is characterized by impulsiveness and mindlessness. Guard against hasty thinking with *intentional thinking*. (b) Narrow thinking includes my-side bias and thinking in patterns from the past. Guard against narrow thinking with *comprehensive thinking*. (c) Fuzzy thinking refers to problems of clarity and precision, and tends to overgeneralize. Guard against fuzzy thinking with *facilitative thinking*. (d) Sprawling thinking wanders endlessly in a disorganized way. One thought leads to another and yet to another in crazy-quilt manner. Guard against sprawling thinking with *focused enthusiasm*.

If we are to work wiser, our thinking has to go beyond the defaults that come easily. Default thinking leaves us working harder, while working wiser requires that we shift our thinking to be intentional, comprehensive, facilitative and focused.

Guard Symbols

> *A medical equipment company displayed large photographs of all the types of machinery it produced. A visiting consultant wandering the halls observed the display and thought about the employees in the company. "Have you considered displaying photographs of people whose lives are saved by this equipment?" she asked. It was a good question about what the company was communicating. Not long after this observation the machinery pictures were replaced with photos of the men, women and children who had benefited from use of the equipment. A different sense of purpose, passion and energy now infused the company. The pictures became a symbol for all the human beings served by the company – not machinery.*

People are more likely to be energized when a positive symbol of the purpose and working "on behalf of" is clear. As in the case above, machinery ceases to be machinery and becomes a life-giving necessity.

Symbols Are Key

What are the symbolic statements you see and hear in your workplace? Do pictures, charts or timelines signal that learning is taking place? In projects, annual reports or events, what indicates that you are learning with intentionality and care? What symbols are representing your values, purpose, intent and context?

"Lifelong learning" is becoming a slogan in many organizations. A slogan such as "car of the year," "we are #1" or "quality is our job" is the verbal equivalent of a symbol, and serves a similar function.

Think about what symbolizes who you are. What is in your office that represents what is important to you? Perhaps a chart of your department's plan on the wall symbolizes your role as a manager, or your favorite quote posted in your office, or your child's drawing pinned up by your computer.

You become a symbol of "thinking and acting together" as you model lifelong learning.

Foster a Climate of Trust

**"Bring multiple perspectives together and examine them.
That's how real learning takes place."
– Daniel Yankelovich[6]**

Intensify Creative Tension

In a learning environment, tension is critical. The creative
tension between a picture of the future (vision) and an audit of
the present (reality) gives a new urgency to choice for actions.
Tension generates power, as facts and feelings provide detail
and shared experiences. From this power flows rich discussions that can lead to
innovative breakthroughs.

We choose between the present and the future to implement action.
"What" and "why" give new meaning to "how." Facts and feelings give critical
depth to discussions. No longer are questions of why and the concerns for the
future the responsibility of just higher management. No longer are feelings
and experiences ignored. Intensifying these tensions with a foundation of
shared values and purpose creates teams. It is in these teams that we have the
opportunity to learn from each other as we share insights about "how" to do
the project and about what is important to us in our shared values.

Pay Attention to Learning Styles

Within a learning organization, learning is captured when we pay attention
to how people process information. Find out which of the five senses is their
preferred learning style: visual (seeing), auditory (hearing), or kinesthetic
(touching, smelling, tasting).[7] A visual learner retains information through
images and pictures. An auditory learner remembers words and sequences.
Finally, a kinesthetic learner recalls information through physical sensations.
Paying attention to these learning styles helps everyone on the team to be
engaged and to capture learning.

Figure 1 (page 162) clarifies behavioral indicators[8] that can help us infor-
mally assess the preferred style of each team member.

Facilitative Approach

Behavioral Indicators of Optimum Learning Styles

Visual	Auditory	Kinesthetic
Organized	Talks to self	Likes physical rewards
Neat & orderly	Easily distracted	Touches people and stands close
More deliberate	Learns by listening	Moves a lot
Memorizes by pictures	Memorizes by steps, sequence, procedures	Learns by doing
Less distracted by noise	Verbalizes alternatives	Memorizes by moving
Has trouble remembering verbal instruction	Remembers what was discussed	Learns through entertainment
Wants overall view and purpose; cautious	May monopolize conversation	Remembers impressions
Remembers what is seen	Remembers from beginning to end	Uses action words, talks with gestures
Sees words when spelling	Makes sounds that portray images	Likes action books; reflects actions with own body
Uses vivid imagery		Acts images out

Figure 1

Based on the indicators listed in Figure 1, three modes of learning are used in accessing information.

- Visual learners need visual imagery and written concepts:
    - words like "see," "look" and "picture this"
    - graphic presentations
    - pictures, images and visual descriptions
    - presentation of a drawn model and then a quiet period for thinking
- Auditory learners need sound bites as well as questions:
    - spoken logic
    - discussions
    - precise and narrative descriptions
    - metaphors and stories

- Kinesthetic learners need activities and movement:
  - lower and slower tone of voice
  - metaphors
  - permission to remain silent
  - demonstration and hands-on teaching

Although everyone employs some aspects of each learning style, we grasp, remember and implement concepts easier and more quickly if they are presented in a manner that is consistent with our preferred style.

Use some aspect of all three learning styles in every meeting or event to show respect for individual learning styles. Trust builds when our messages and behaviors value individual differences.

Strengthen Communication Loops

As the chief operating officer of a not-for-profit organization, Melissa built a strong operational leadership team. The organization grew tenfold almost overnight when they procured a new contract. Attempts to orchestrate the various systems necessary to manage this growth eventually reached a state of crisis. When the organization's capacity to meet performance and financial goals deteriorated, it was clear that a new plan of action was needed. The challenge for Melissa was to ensure that action was strategic, timely and endorsed by the executive team and board of the organization.

Melissa engaged TeamTech to assist her and her team in leading the organization through this tough challenge. They met or communicated daily as mentor, coach and sounding board.

First, an overall course of action for the organization's turnaround was established, and critical communication bridges were created with executive leadership.

Melissa expanded her knowledge and understanding of financial state-ments and trends. Her authority to ask for information and assume a role she had not previously played was validated as she communicated with executive leadership.

Melissa also assessed the capacity of operations in an effort to take advantage of strengths and to supplement and address weaknesses. She and her team thought through questions that broadened and deepened thinking so actions became more strategic. Among other things, in this process they tested assump-

tions about important leadership issues and decisions. Strategies were validated and questions asked to ensure thinking was as comprehensive as possible.

Organizational energy focused on ensuring the organization's survival. The team responded with clarity on how to move forward in the midst of daily uncertainty and organizational crisis. The organization's turnaround succeeded and was expedited due to the strengthened communication loops between team members, executive leadership and the financial structures of the organization.

Melissa and her team built in accountability to timelines and fast-tracked performance. Her reflection was, "In three months of working together we stopped the negative drain on assets and ensured the organization's continuing viability."

In spite of information-age technology, communication problems persist. Underneath all the "need to know" policies and communication channels lies a deeper concern: "Am I in or out of the communication loop?"

When people are out of the loop, they:

- feel irrelevant and not trusted
- may become suspicious of those "in the loop"
- may believe that they are unworthy
- translate this perspective by reducing their involvement, motivation and passion and have an increasingly cynical view

When people feel they are in the (communication) loop, they:

- feel a sense of worthiness and respect
- feel that "we are in this together"
- believe they have something valuable to give to the team and organization
- act with confidence, creativity and purpose

Help people feel that they are in the loop, by trusting intuition, observing and listening closely for the kinds of communication people need.

- When someone asks questions about a given situation, ask yourself if he or she needs to be in the loop.
- Keep the people who authorized a given effort up-to-date. When informed, they will worry less and be more relaxed and will provide valuable insight.
- When an issue or topic is sensitive, use face-to-face communication.

- Capture the details in writing. When necessary, check for clarity and understanding using face-to-face communication.
- Communicate to the team as a whole to save time and minimize misunderstandings. Take the time to ask the team what they heard being communicated. If needed, deepen the communication by asking reflective questions. "What concerns does this raise?" "What possibilities do you see?" "What have we learned?"

Let the following seven critical guidelines shape your communication so your messages are consistent, comprehensive and on target.

1. **Stick with the big picture.** Keep your message consistent with the big picture. Prepare your communication with all the organizational dynamics in mind. As a result, your communication will be more intentional and will energize the team's thinking and acting.

2. **Be purposeful.** Know the purpose of the task/team/department. Stay true to the purpose. Emphasize and share the purpose – live the purpose.

3. **Encourage ownership.** Shape your message so it allows/encourages others to step up and take ownership (e.g., If someone exhibits passion for an idea, your communication needs to support them in taking the lead to "make it happen").

4. **Invite inquiry.** Open the door for questions in your communication. Continually invite reflection in your message.

5. **Recognize the team.** Look for and recognize the team. Communicate the role, benefits and expectations of the team. Be mindful of times when all team members need to hear the information at the same time.

6. **Nurture the innovator.** Communicate the challenge list, share innovative ideas, encourage the creative and share information that can help others do their job.

7. **Build consensus.** Communicate with "moving together" in mind. Share information so people can operate in and further mold the consensus.

Stabilize Information

If information is complex, or if group members have lost energy, information tends to wander around in the brain looking for a file cabinet. "Mark off" the information so that it is stabilized or remembered appropriately in people's thinking by:

- putting the information in large, neat, consistent words on a white board
- looking at the written words, not the person or group, and pausing long enough for people to process the information
- asking a confirmation question, "Is this it?"
- continuing with the meeting or workshop.[9]

Communication is not just a matter of what you say or intend but what the other person understands.

If there is incongruity between the verbal and the nonverbal, the nonverbal will have a greater influence. Nonverbal communication aids long-term retention of learning so that what is learned can be used on the job. To increase your speaking effectively, use a nonverbal pause as attention is caught by the pause. The words spoken immediately after a pause are marked off for long term memory, which stabilizes the wealth of information you have been sharing.

Select Thinking Mode

Another key to strengthening the communication loop is setting the framework for the type of thinking needed. Each of the nine modes of thinking in Figure 2 is unique. You can use more than one mode at a time when thinking together. When thinking gets off track, pull it back by reminding team members of which thinking mode they agreed to use when they started the process.

Catalyze Learning

"We must be the change we want to see in the world."
– Mahatma Ghandi

Create a Safe Zone

To stay competitive, many of us are trying to reverse one hundred years of business tradition that taught us to function

How-to Action

Thinking Modes

Mode	When to Use	How to Get Started
1. Model building Creating an image or plan of what is needed, including steps, timeframes, people involved, etc.	When many options exist. Build models you can pilot (try out), then learn everything you can from the pilot.	Identify together the constraints each model must consider. Ask people to work in small teams to build their model.
2. Problem-solving Figuring out how to get from A to B when no immediate path is obvious.	When you are stuck and need a new approach or new thinking on a particular situation.	Begin by having team members share what is known and unknown. Also share questions and concerns. Ask the team what all this means for what is needed next.
3. "Blue sky" thinking Free-form thinking in which every crazy idea, option and possibility is welcome.	When you need breakthroughs.	Remind people that anything goes. Either throw out a new idea or build on one already shared.
4. "What if ...?" thinking Forecasting the likely consequences of actions.	When you need to think through different scenarios of the future.	Begin with one possible scenario and create several more. For each assumption ask, "What if?"
5. Knowledge gathering Detecting and defining the gaps, data and experiences relevant to the situation.	When you need more information.	Start with what is known (data + experiences). Think together about what else needs to be known and why.
6. Sharing insights Thinking together in order to uncover the meaning/implications of data, events, situations.	When reflection on the topic is required.	Get the data and information in front of the team. Facilitate a conversation to uncover insights. If there are a lot of data, consider (first) grouping the data into common themes.
7. Analyzing Evaluating, critiquing and examining information to find the strengths and weaknesses.	When the situation needs to be thought through carefully, clarifying relevance, cost (human & financial), etc.	Talk through the situation. Begin with questions of clarity. Ask people to share strengths they see and explore why they are strengths. Repeat for weaknesses/concerns.
8. Creating strategy Thinking ahead to determine the next steps.	When you desire implementation.	Think together first to identify the blocks. Strategies are most effective when they work on removing blocks to getting done what is needed.
9. Decision-making Finding and choosing between alternatives.	When a choice needs to be made.	First, facilitate people's thinking through facts, feelings and experiences. Then ask for implications. Finally, ask people based on what they heard to state the decision they understand "we" are making.

Figure 2

in a top-down organization. We are trying to shift our attitudes toward people, from "watching" them to helping them manage themselves. We accomplish this by learning to think and act differently.

After the World Trade Center tragedy the wisdom of many leaders distilled "into four basic truisms about being a manager: be calm, tell the truth, put people before business, then get back to business as soon as possible." [10] Even though that situation was unprecedented, those management truisms help us know how to work together.

A safe zone is created when we encourage and create occasions for people to talk, think and act together. An atmosphere of resolve, creativity, acceptance and fun allows learning opportunities to flourish. Fostering a climate of sharing and reflection expands and deepens relationships and connections.

> During the 1976 USA bicentennial celebrations the Institute of Cultural Affairs (ICA) facilitated a town meeting in every county across the nation. At daylong meetings people tackled the question of what they wanted the community to look like in the future. At the end of the meetings, in most counties, the same comment was heard: "Those two haven't talked to each other in years! They've fought forever over the parks (etc.). How did you get them to talk together?"
>
> It seemed like magic. The format that orchestrated the interactions and generated reflection created the safe zone of the town meeting. This is what allowed people to raise questions of the future and discuss them without dissolving into arguments. When people share, they discover that they can learn from each other and work together.

New times demand new skills. Leadership is being recast. Leadership is not a position, it is a mindset. It challenges us to operate daily with decision, energy and passion. The complexity of the Information Age demands that each of us exercise the responsibility of leadership in our sphere of influence. We can no longer be content for many to follow while few lead. Everyone a leader®[11] is not some utopian dream, but a practical answer.

Choose to Be a Facilitative Leader

Don't wait for someone to ask you to take responsibility. Choose to lead now. Don't wait to be trained; develop yourself now. There is a dramatic growth in the demand for facilitative leadership throughout organizations. This may not be in your "job description," but you can make this choice and experience more work satisfaction.

Based on 1,200 responses from executives participating in Conference Board Councils, it was discovered that "top executives' worries about developing future leaders has become the hottest topic at business meetings. (Percentage of meetings in which leadership was addressed: in 2001, fifty-four percent – in 2002, that percentage increased to sixty-two percent)."[12]

> **Success in the transition from "a few leaders" to "everyone a leader" requires unlearning the old leadership paradigm and learning a new one.**

Challenging the norm is key to this learning. In the process of unlearning and learning, any inconsistency can cause a return to a former belief. Examine the following areas to determine if your actions and messages are telling a story about the new leadership paradigm.

- Space – is it encouraging horizontal communication? Is the workplace configured so that it conveys the purpose, values and mission of the organization?
- Information systems – do they deliver the images people need to hear? Are all the information systems communicating more than just data and indicating why the data are important?

Cultivate a Compelling Story

What we see and hear in the workplace helps form our self-talk. Everybody talks to him/herself. We do it at a fierce pace inside our heads. Our self-talk constantly reminds us of our beliefs and experiences. Whenever we change the way we respond to situations, we are changing our self-talk – the compelling story – about a given situation.

A compelling story tells people what they are doing and why and gives purpose to their team, project or organization by giving life and spirit to everyday activities. "Storying" helps people see their work inside a larger picture of what needs to be done and provides motivation.

A familiar story illustrates the benefit of a compelling story. Two stone masons were laying stone for a church some time in the middle ages. "What are you doing?" asked a young boy. "I am laying stones," responded one. "I am building a cathedral," said the other.

Their answers were very revealing: the first stone mason was doing a job. The other was fulfilling a purpose, convinced that what he was doing was completely necessary and totally worthwhile. He was a cathedral builder. Which of these two individuals would you like working with you?

How do you help yourself and others develop this kind of clear, compelling story? A story that provides you with an identity (i.e., cathedral builder) motivates you daily by giving you an identity.

Think for a moment of some of the compelling stories that have shaped the identity of organizations and the people involved in them.

Disney: "Out to make people happy."

Boeing: "Committed to push the envelope of aerodynamic technology."

NASA: "Put a man on the moon by the end of the decade."

Take this a step further. In the midst of constant complex change, the story changes. What are the signals that tell you the story has changed or perhaps is just plain missing?

- Constantly referring to the "good old days"
- Struggling to cooperate
- Resisting anything new
- Skeptical of management
- "Just putting in the time"

To overcome these attitudes, a new story needs to be created and cultivated. If who people understand themselves to be and what they are about has changed, they may need help in forging a new story.

A story is a verbal/visual picture that "makes sense" of what is going on by building a cohesive whole instead of isolated (fragmented) activities. It gives meaning to data, organizes information, taps into emotions and, thus, allows learning to take place.

Making sense of things motivates individuals and groups by giving them a directional map of where they are and where they are going in the larger scheme of things.

"Story" the purpose so everyone is on the same page. The story about "what" people are doing and "why" highlights the purpose of a team, project or organization. These stories shape what people do, how they do it and what they learn from their efforts.

"Businesses, communities and people will thrive on the basis of their stories, not just on data and information," according to Rolf Jensen in *The Dream Society.* "Nike sells youth, success, fame and triumph. Rolex sells a story of affluence. Disney is perhaps the best at selling dreams."[13]

A good story gives birth to other stories and prompts deeper reflection. Storytelling transforms experiences and allows learning to emerge. Stories have an emotional trigger and are stored in long-term memory.

You get stopped in the hallway by Sienna, one of your associates from the accounting department. She is upset because the group you chair is working to show individuals the organization's financial results so they can make better decisions. Sienna is concerned that sharing financial information will result in competitors getting the information and employees asking for more money. As you listen to Sienna, you sense she is limited in her view of "the level of involvement the organization needs." You know that you can strengthen the image of a new story.

You decide to build images in the story of what is needed.

• New images about "the level of involvement the organization needs"

You stress the need for informed decision-making at all levels of the organization. Financial information is part of the critical information decision-makers need.

• New images about "what the marketplace demands"

You know today's changing marketplace demands that the organization have more people thinking and acting as owners. Owners know the financial impact of their decisions.

• New images about "who you are"

You help Sienna see herself as a teacher as well as a protector of the financial assets of the organization. You sustain these new images to reinforce a new story by:

- *Encouraging regular meetings with employees, asking these customers how the financial information has been helpful to them.*
- *Continuing to ask Sienna where she is having success as a teacher of financial information, where she is struggling and what she is learning.*
- *Link Sienna with people from the training and development department to help her develop and improve her teaching and consulting skills.*

Organizations need people who are committed to the mission. You can pull people together by creating a common story of what "we" are about (mission/purpose) and sustain it with a powerful symbol. Here are five points for creating a common story and symbol with indicators to tell you when you have been successful.

1. **Answer the question of "why?"** Why has been answered when the purpose is clear, the implications are obvious and people are taking action.
2. **Discover a sound bite to capture the meaning.** You have a sound bite when people communicate the mission in a few words (i.e., "A man on the moon by the end of the decade.").
3. **Picture how our story of who we are and why will change the way things work.** The picture is real when the "mission" becomes bigger than the "job." People work together to get things done.
4. **State the benefits to fire the imagination.** The benefits have fired the imagination when people can share succinct statements about why a particular task or situation is so important.
5. **Invent symbols that reflect the purpose.** A symbol has emerged when it is seen in all the practical everyday things that people do.

Three kinds of stories can "make sense" of things for a group:
- Funny stories – pick up the energy of the group and release a new sense of momentum.
- Frustrating stories – create a new empathy so people experience "We're in this together."
- Meaningful stories – give pause and provide time for reflecting on what is important so true learning can take place.

Use a team process to create a story, symbol and sound bite with a visual and audible expression of the team's identity. This reminds team members why they exist and where they are trying to go.

1. As a team:
- **Pull from the PAST**
  Where we have been –
  - review events
  - reexamine issues
  - remember situations
  - recall experiences
  - review the history of the organization and team

- **Say "YES" to the PRESENT**
  Where we are –
    - rehearse purpose
    - listen to perspectives
    - recognize driving forces
    - acknowledge what it will take to move into the future
    - discuss current projects
    - explore relationships to other teams/organizations
- **Announce the FUTURE**
  Where we are going –
    - project direction
    - state what will be accomplished in the future
    - discuss possibilities opening up
    - review changes foreseen in the future

For all three stages (past, present and future), brainstorm ideas and phrases and use them to help spark people's thinking. What is really important in each for the team and/or organization? What has, is or will contribute to defining our purpose?

2. Review the images. Add other images or ideas people have.
3. Ask the team to reflect on the images.
   "Which images caught your attention?"
   "What did we say that you had not remembered or not thought about?"
   "Which images trigger stories and why?"
4. Using these images, brainstorm sound bites. A sound bite is a few words that capture what the team is about ... the purpose (i.e., "Be the best we can be"). Select one sound bite.
5. Brainstorm possible visual symbols suggested by the images and the sound bite. Working individually, sketch some symbols and put them on the wall. Notice which ones catch the attention and imagination of the team. Decide on the most exciting and appropriate symbol. Make suggestions on how to refine it, perhaps combining elements from several sketches. Assign two or three people to do the final drawing.
6. While the final drawing is being made, discuss the story that the images, symbol and sound bite tell. Ask, "As you've listened to all that has been said, what is the story you would tell about this team?" Ask several

people to respond. Assign three or four people to write the story on behalf of the team.

7. As a team, discuss the practical ways you can use the symbol, sound bite and story as both visual and verbal reminders of who the team is and the decisions that have been made.

8. Reflect on the entire process by asking ...
   "What did we do?"
   "What was surprising/a struggle for you?"
   "Why is this important?"
   "What will this story, sound bite and symbol do for us?

The story template is illustrated in Figure 3.

During the story building process, steer away from ...

- downplaying how you got to where you are
- a negative focus
- cynicism
- trying to force or rush a story ... allow time to think about who the team really is and who they really want to become
- being too factual and pragmatic ... let the poetic imagination freely flow.

The Story Template

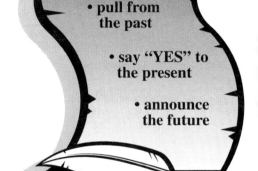

- pull from the past
- say "YES" to the present
- announce the future

Figure 3

> **"If the human body is 'what we eat,'
> then our organizations become the stories we tell ourselves."
> – Peter Senge[14]**

Dead-End Stories

In contrast to a compelling story, which releases energy, sparks momentum and motivates for action, a dead-end story brings momentum to a screeching halt. Almost nothing stops action faster than a dead-end story. Which of these dead-end stories do you hear in your workplace?

"We can't …"   "They won't …"
"It is always a problem when …"   "He is an underperformer."
"This is impossible to do."   "They are always late."
"No one seems to care."   "Been there, done that."
"I have no time."   "We have no support."

Dead-end stories demotivate. They share three characteristics:

1. Judgmental language, blaming situations or complaining attitude:
   "There is a bad morale problem here." "Everyone is so negative."
2. A negative relationship, sustaining problems or trapping cynicism: "We have chronic underperformers." "They just don't understand."
3. An unwillingness to move forward: "We can't." "I'm stopped, I don't know what to do.

You may recognize a dead-end story – in yourself or in another person – in a meeting, informal conversation, or other interaction. Work to flip the story and turn it around by using some of the following suggestions.

1. Objectify the situation

Ask for objective information so you can acknowledge the real problem.

- What are people doing? (*facts*)
- What are people saying? (*facts*)
- What continues to happen now? (*facts*)
- What happened in the past? (*feelings/experiences*)
- What has led you to this conclusion? (*implications*)

Encourage clear language about what is seen and heard, and be precise about time and place without (positive or negative) interpretation.

Examples of objectifying the situation:

"No one has stepped up to take responsibility in this project."
"He came to the staff meeting without a report."

Ask: "What have you seen or heard that makes you say this?"

The objective situation is: Three weeks after the task assignment, no one has anything to report.

2. Find a turnaround clue

Look for a "turnaround clue" to help separate issues and emotions. Listen for or ask, "What is this really about?"

Turnaround clues are structures or processes that are neutral or nonjudgmental categories like

a meeting	a procedure
a relationship	a role
purpose	information
performance	an attitude
communication	an expectation

In the example above of "objectifying the situation," the turnaround clue is "task assignment."

When you find the clue, have a conversation to verify that the turnaround clue is the real issue.

> "So this is about the expectations of the team?"
> "You are talking about the information from yesterday's meeting?"
> "This is about our weekly meetings?"
> "Is this about the role John is playing?"

If the person says, "No," then ask, "What's underneath this?" Or give choices, "Is this more about the need to communicate or more about the task being unclear?" Continue the conversation until you are clear on which neutral category is at the crux of the dead-end story.

3. Restart the story

Ask questions that probe what the person involved is going to do. Help build images of how to be responsible in the situation. Add an action verb and a descriptive adjective to the turnaround clue so there is a shift to future thinking, opening the possibility of moving forward.

> " … So the issue is about creating different working relationships."
> " … So the frustration can be addressed by developing new focused meeting agendas."
> " … It sounds like we need to set performance expectations."

The chart in Figure 4 lists turnaround clues, action verbs and descriptive adjectives to use in restarting a dead-end story.

Thinkabouts in Dealing with Dead-End Stories

- Don't try to fix the dead-end story when the story is at the height of resistance. Trying to "fix it" will drive the person to hold onto the story even tighter. Instead, get

Thinkabout

176

Flipping Dead-End Stories

Turnaround Clues		Action Verbs		Descriptive Adjectives	
Ability	Meetings	accelerating	fostering	appropriate	focused
Accountability	Performance	assigning	honoring	decreased	increased
Attitude	Policies	creating	prioritizing	different	new
Communication	Procedures	changing	promoting	different working	technical
Customer service	Technology	delegating	rethinking	effective	sequential
Decision-making	Training	developing	setting	energetic	relevant
Evaluations	Priorities	establishing		expanded	
Expectations	Purpose				
Goals	Relationships				
Information	Roles				
Involvement	Values				

Figure 4

the problem repositioned by asking questions that provide clues to what is really troubling the person (e.g., "You are worried about the computer software?") so the person involved is willing to consider options.

- Don't agree with a dead-end story. If you do, your future efforts to flip it will be sabotaged. It is helpful not to say:

  "Yes, they really are a negative group of people."
  "You know, I've noticed that too. It just doesn't seem to change."
  "Absolutely! If only they would …"

- Flip a dead-end story so the problem that triggered it can be solved. But you do not want to flip a dead-end story when:

  – You perceive the person is just "blowing off steam" and you think he will get the problem solved.
  – If the person is incapable of dealing with any issue (time of high emotion, violence), any response will fuel negativity.

A good story will catalyze learning and allow dead-end perceptions to shift.

When George wanted to ensure momentum in planned actions and capture learnings, he put up a sign by the coffee machine: "We Made It Happen" story time. Join us for drinks and snacks at 4:00 p.m. Friday afternoon. Come with your "We Made It Happen" story."

Everyone was surprised by the energy released when stories led to the discovery of successes and accomplishments.

Nuture Teamhood

"The fundamental learning unit in any organization is a team, not an individual."
– Peter Senge[15]

Self-interest (individualism) sometimes makes acting as a team member difficult. *Webster's Dictionary* defines teamwork as "joint action by a group of people, in which individual interests are subordinated." If being a learning organization is the goal, teamwork is the means.

Teamhood operates "on behalf of" and gives power, not because we like each other but because of our focus on the mission.

Corporate effort is invested in implementing a plan or it is just another set of good ideas. Meetings are for the sake of achieving task outcomes and accountability is in the context of the corporate task.

The teamhood or "on behalf of" stance (e.g., working for the common good of the group, not your individual preference):

- calls forth each person's insights for the wisest result
- ensures that everyone gets to hear and be heard
- opens up new choices
- enables us to challenge old assumptions

Team-building exercises are often done to build a team, but it is the focus on the task (thinking and acting together) that makes the difference in creating a team.

Carl's team has been sent to a one-day training on a newly required service technique. Several members of the team are annoyed at having to spend the day in this training.

Carl is surprised to see three members pull back, joke and talk about unrelated work. Not only are they being disruptive, they are ignoring the information presented about the new service technique. Carl, on the other hand, is intent on learning as much as possible about the technique. He begins to consider how he can shift his team's participation to be more engaged in learning.

He knows he won't have much time. During the morning break, he approaches them in the hall and reminds them about the service contract they just received. Then he reveals his ideas of the role the new technique will play in daily operations. After expressing his concern about not being able to learn all he needs today, Carl asks for their comments, "What is your understanding of the importance of this service technique? As you've thought about it, do you think it will help us or slow us down?"

"My expectation is that it will give me some different ways to complete my work. What are you expecting from this new technique?" he asks.

Several in the group begin responding to Carl's questions. Returning from the break, team members speak in quieter tones and begin to share insights.

The team shifts its stance after Carl describes the larger picture on issues, benefits and expectations. Team members are able to get smarter because they decide to listen and learn for the benefit of the team.

One more change in their workplace procedures faced Carl and his coworkers. The struggle was how to accept, learn about and work with the changes. We can anticipate more change in the first decade of the twenty-first century than in all of the previous fifty years! To handle this perpetual and accelerating change we need new ways of thinking. We have to employ the tools that let us operate with a systems perspective, in-depth reflection and an ability to capture learning at every opportunity.

In order to catalyze and capture learning, cultivate the collegiality that fosters knowledge sharing. Every time you gather as a team, tie together where the group has been and where it is going, so that people see their highs and lows within the framework of a journey rather than random, unrelated activities.

Use the four steps of ALPS (pages 145-149) to model consistency and alignment in day-to-day actions.

- Create Awareness – wake up people to their own potential to make a difference
- Generate Learning – make sure that people have the knowledge, tools and capabilities to make a difference
- Encourage Pilots – enable people to try out ideas and projects to discover how to make a difference
- Practice Sharing – encourage people to exchange discoveries and learnings to spread success

Summary

Learning is a continuous journey of discovery. Being a "learning organization" is an image – a symbol – toward which many strive. While there are no simple answers for how to get there the following are helpful guidelines.

Build a climate of trust by strengthening communication loops. Catalyze learning opportunities and cultivate a compelling story to illustrate what the team is about. Focus capabilities to make a difference on the team as well as on the individual. Cultivate teamhood to release the power of learning.

What It Takes

**"We start as fools and become wise through experience."
– African Proverb**

The Facilitative Journey

The decision to be a facilitative leader takes you on a journey, sometimes over unknown terrain. The Facilitative Advantage Map (Figure 1, page 182) illustrates the thinking process necessary for the journey. Consider what the group needs to reach its outcome. Screen (read) what you know about the people and the situation, then decide on appropriate methods to invite people to think and act together.

When planning a family road trip from Kansas City to Omaha, I studied the Nebraska map and considered the intent of the journey. Did we need to know the fastest route, the most scenic route, the route with the best restaurants? Did we need to experience a leisurely, explore-the-countryside type of trip? Or did we need to experience a swift, no-stop, lets-get-there drive?

I thought about some of the stresses that the family had experienced in the past on long car trips (screening) and decided to try the scenic route for a relaxing, leisurely day.

Next, to focus on the situation, I thought about previous family car trips: everyone's level of participation; whether they had connected with what we were doing; and how the passengers had acted during the drive. I thought about the things the family could do during the daytrip. In preparation, I packed in-car games for the two children, studied the map for fun places to stop along the way and brought a special picnic lunch (methods).

We arrived in Omaha in the late afternoon after a refreshing and fun day with scenic stops and a fun picnic at the playground.

Thinking about how to be facilitative for the success of a family outing is not unlike being facilitative in a workplace setting.

The Facilitative Advantage™ Map

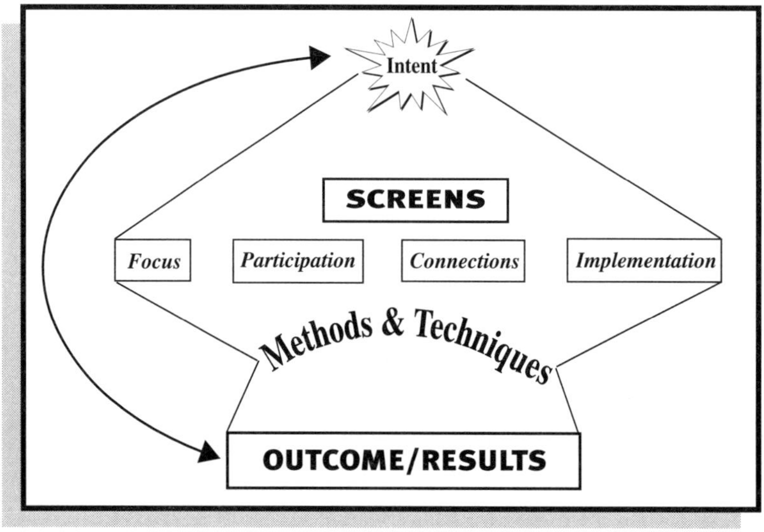

Figure 1

Screen for Clarity

The starting point for acting facilitatively is finding out what you need to know about the people involved. The following screens are useful in clarifying what you observe by revealing the subtle details that make the difference in being facilitative and strategic.

1. **Screen for focus**

   Focus clarifies the purpose so things make sense, maximizes the effective use of people's time, encourages action and indicates whether or not the "right" problem is identified.

With focus, there is alignment, not fragmentation. Ask yourself:

"Do people share a common purpose?"

"Do they know how the purpose affects them?"

"Do they believe the outcome is important?"

"Are people willing to consider what is being presented or discussed and willing to make decisions?"

2. **Screen for participation**

Participation creates more knowledge, develops stronger ownership, facilitates quicker responses and solves more problems.

With participation, there is responsibility, not defensiveness. Ask yourself:

"Are people ready to commit the time?"

"Are they willing to share ideas?"

"Are they receptive to being challenged by others?"

"Are people contributing ideas and applications, either individually or as a group?"

"Are they participating as a team or as individuals?"

3. **Screen for connections**

Connections release insights, sustain motivation and passion, and spark responsibility.

Connections create relationships, not isolation. Ask yourself:

"Are people building on others' ideas?"

"Are they asking for the bigger picture?"

"Are they seeing the need to link together (people and/or ideas)?"

"What do you see and hear in people's reactions to you, to others, to an issue, to the task?"

4. **Screen for implementation**

Implementation determines effective operations, employee buy-in, customer satisfaction and walking the talk.

Implementation invites movement, not inertia. Ask yourself:

"Are people taking action?"

"Are they building timelines?"

"Are they reallocating time, energy and resources to make it happen?"

Choose Methods and Techniques

Learn from your observations and experiences and think through methods and techniques for effective interactions. The key is choosing the right method or technique for the right time. Examine the desired outcome and your intent (what you conclude the group needs to know and experience to accomplish the outcome) to determine effective methods and/or techniques.

Taking time to reflect as a group may seem like a luxury you can't afford. But the truth is that taking time to think through an issue or action together usually saves time in the long run.

Design the process, create a supportive atmosphere and set an appropriate context (see pages 66-70) for details on how to do so). Ask reflective questions to explore what the data mean.

"What is important here?"

"What makes sense for this situation?"

"Where are we likely to run into problems?"

"What is needed?"

"What is new for people?"

"What is the largest context?"

A large state social service agency with more than 6,000 employees and an operating budget of $1.8 billion is challenged to streamline its operations. The state budget crisis intensifies the challenge presented to the agency and its leadership. It is necessary to integrate programs and for staff members to partner with the larger community.

The agency's leader and her executive team believe that the capacity to be strategic and facilitative is a critical competency that can help the agency continue to meet growing service needs with fewer dollars and people. Further, she and the team want to model a new leadership style.

The leader and her team commit to a program designed to increase their strategic facilitation skills. The program includes eight training sessions to focus the team on:

• Strategic processes that help people hold the relationship between the task at hand and the big picture.

• Facilitative/reflective processes that achieve the act of thinking and taking action together. (These are critical skills when managing a tightening fiscal situation, staff reductions and vocal stakeholders.)

A monthly practicum helped them apply newly acquired strategic, reflective and facilitative skills to upcoming meetings, decisions and problem-solving sessions. These practica provided opportunity for:

1. Detailed planning and preparation

2. Facilitation practice and coaching

3. On-site observations and direct feedback

4. Feedback and professional development

The team learned to strategically manage everyday crises rather than allowing these crises to manage them. Their learning led to new strategic facilitation skills, including:

1. Big-picture thinking so that all the dynamics at play can be identified and a strategic response developed.

2. Being intentional about what people need to know and experience to make good decisions and achieve a desired outcome.

3. Building a shared vision so employees and stakeholders can see the practical next steps that need to be taken.

4. Facilitating meetings that demonstrate effective communication and collaborations.

What a Facilitative Leader Looks Like

"At first, there is no road; it is only when one person begins it that others see it."
– Chinese Proverb

Set the Tone with Attitude

As a facilitative leader, your attitude and demeanor set the tone and send a signal to the group. The **Four P's** in both your attitude and your words will shape the message you send to others:

1. Be **P**ositive. See new possibilities, imagine a diverse range of possibilities, have courage and be willing to take risks. In your words express: "Let's do whatever it takes." "What is the opportunity here?" "We can do it."

2. Be **P**ersistent. Every day think about what is needed in every situation. Rehearse your desired future, take responsibility for your choices, and have a driving curiosity. In your words express: "Where can we have an

impact?" "What if … what if … what if?" "What do we want in this situation?"

3. Be **P**assionate. Do something for the sheer pleasure of doing it, enjoy what you are doing, and experience work as a labor of love. In your words express: "In terms of this project, here's where I'd like to put my energy." "What is keeping your interest here?" "What do you think is important?"

4. Be **P**resent. Anticipate the future and learn from the past. Live in the present, and be honest about what you have. In your words express: "What are we doing now?" "Are we being honest with ourselves?" "What do our present choices say about what is important?"

The concept of leadership has changed from a position to a mindset. Each of us can choose to exercise the responsibility of leadership in our sphere of influence. "Everyone a leader®[1] is a practical solution to the quest for new ideas and new practices.

Recognize Vulnerability as a Strength

Managers are increasingly changing their supervising style and taking a more facilitative approach. At the same time employees are depending less on the traditional hierarchy and their job description, and are starting to do whatever it takes to create quality services and innovative products. This is a radical departure from the past.

With a learner mindset you have the courage, and also the vulnerability, to change, to be an innovator, to facilitate learning. One way to experience vulnerability as a strength is to recall times when you were at risk; perhaps you moved, took a new job, made your first presentation, chaired an important meeting. Take a few minutes to think about the following questions and learn from past experience.

Reflective Learning

"What was the situation?"
"What do you remember about that time?"
"Who was involved?"
"What about that situation seemed risky?"
"What did you gain?"
"What did you lose?"
"How would you describe your experience of being vulnerable?"

"How did that experience become a strength for you?

Communication and learning thrive when we experiment, when we risk being wrong, when we take a chance without knowing the result. Asking questions, admitting you don't know everything and publicly stating that the proposed solution may not be the best one dramatically increases vulnerability and learning at the same time. Learn to recognize vulnerability as an asset and strength in order to say "yes" to situations of uncertainty and creativity.

This new environment is risky for everyone.

Practice Personal Disciplines

Your own personal disciplines are as important – or more so – than the skills, techniques and methods you use as a facilitative leader. Practice the interior qualities that are the personal disciplines of a facilitator outlined by Jon and Maureen Jenkins.[2]

Detachment: let go of your own personal needs and continually reexamine what you are deciding.

Engagement: call into question what is going on and accept responsibility for the group to achieve what is needed.

Focus: keep who you are in alignment with who the group is; make choices and know why.

Interior Dialogue: pay attention to the chorus of voices and influences that surrounds you.

Intentionality: be clear about the meaning of what you do; focus your expenditure of energy.

Wonder: be a friend of the unexpected; appreciate the mystery, depth and greatness of your colleagues.

Awareness: sharpen the observation of details and the whole.

Integrity: imagine the best future possible for the group; rehearse the future before it happens.

Action: assume risks to keep your own spirit and ethical fabric in peak form; practice decisiveness and commitment.

Ask yourself, "What special value do I add?" "Am I willing to think about projects, purpose or contribution of tasks after work hours?"

Act Out the Four C's

Acting out facilitative leadership calls for care, corporateness, courage and creativity as defined below.

Care: You embrace the whole and the details. When you shift from traditional concern to comprehensive care, you focus on the structures, processes and people. You look for ways to target your care to deal with problems effectively.

Corporateness: You know that teamwork is necessary to release action. You believe that people want to do their best. You work for the common good with your colleagues, knowing that together you are more than the sum of the parts. You experience a shift from individual authority to team leadership.

Courage: You have the courage to unlearn and learn. Your courage is personal, but the organization can help in two ways: when you are confident of support in the organization and when you experience the support of your peers undergoing the same change. You are open to self-examination. You are willing to play with ideas that may seem wrong. You decide what is important to be effective and sustain engagement. The question is, what is needed, not what do I want? Courage is not stoic endurance, but a lifelong resolve to be engaged.

Creativity: You employ your gifts to shape plans practically. You make sure that structures and systems mirror expectations. You link practical methods to tap the inventiveness of people.

- Do you dare having courage?
- Do you dare risking your own intuitions?
- Do you dare releasing your care and moving on opportunities?

Reflective Learning

Set the Stage for Facilitation

**"Our freedom begins with knowing our intentions,
knowing what matters to us,
knowing which values will guide our actions.
The question, then, is what are we willing to commit to?"
– Peter Block[3]**

Become a Guide

In the Information Age, there are no experts, only students willing to experiment, dream, risk and learn. Choosing to be a facilitative leader allows you to create situations and guide people to new possibilities through what might previously have seemed impossible.

Be a facilitative catalyst, a guide through the processes of thinking and working together. Learn to work smarter and respond proactively with facilitative skills, techniques and methods. Invite others to be facilitative by revealing individual worth, nurturing creativity and capturing passion. Use these skills to step up involvement, deepen understanding and intensify productivity.

When you are helping others to learn, remember Ben Franklin's admonition:
"Tell me and I forget.
Teach me and I remember.
Involve me and I learn."

Constant change is now the norm. Customer demands and global competition are driving the need for internal changes, both organizational and personal.

What is in it for you? More enjoyment in work life, increased levels of employability, new experiences of collegiality and making a difference are the advantages for you personally.

Honor Individuals

When people are valued as human beings, they take on new levels of responsibility. Dr. Gregory S. Berns stated in the *New York Times*, "Scientists have discovered that the small brave act of cooperating with another person, of choosing trust over cynicism, generosity over selfishness, makes the brain light up with quiet joy. It says we're wired to cooperate with each other."[4]

Cooperate with each other by acknowledging, affirming and honoring the contributions of individuals. As you help people focus on the task, the teamwork environment is strengthened. Without teamwork nothing happens. Try the Ten Rules of Order for Century XXI[5] in Figure 2 to develop the interdependence that increases the team's capacity to get things done.

Ten Rules of Order for Century XXI

> "Everyone has wisdom to share.
>
> We need everyone's wisdom for the best result.
>
> The whole picture comes through hearing and understanding all the perspectives.
>
> There are no wrong answers.
>
> The wisdom of the whole is greater than the sum of its parts.
>
> The more people we engage through participation, the wiser we can all become.
>
> Participation blows out our images of what is possible.
>
> People commit to what they create.
>
> The people who implement a plan are the best ones to create the plan.
>
> Participation in planning creates a sense of self-worth, enthusiasm,
>
> respect and accomplishment."
>
> from: "Clashing Images of Participation" by Jo Nelson and
> Brian Stanfield, *Edges*, August, 2000.

Figure 2

These rules can help a learning organization build processes and capabilities that foster team learning using genuine dialogue and sharing of ideas; constant examining of assumptions; systems thinking and shared vision.

Share Values

Shared facilitative beliefs and values help us cooperate with each other and give meaning to what we know as a team/organization.

Figure 3 illustrates a few of the everyday operating values that build trust and the outcomes that result when they are operative.

Everyday Values That Build Trust

Operating Values	What It Looks Like to Operate out of This Value	How This Builds Trust
Customers are #1.	There is quality customer service.	Customer retention is high. Saves time and energy.
There is a clear compelling purpose.	Everyone has insight into what needs to be done.	All work together to accomplish the goal.
Everyone has an important role to play.	People do their own job to the best of their ability.	Individuals are given expanded roles and they trust they will be taken seriously.
There is a spirit of growth.	People are motivated to do the job well.	Relationships are built with the organization as people are knowledgeable to do their job.
People keep learning from each other.	People engage in open communication, sharing of ideas and cross-training.	Confidence is built as people can express their opinions.
People agree on what is important.	What needs to be done is clearly prioritized.	People's judgment is trusted as priorities are done first.

Figure 3

Trust is a by-product and develops – or does not develop – from the values that are revealed in our day-to-day activities. One of the most important conversations today is about values as we do what is important to us. Figure 4 (page 192) shows a pyramid of beliefs and values that we accept as truth when we are operating strategically and being facilitative.

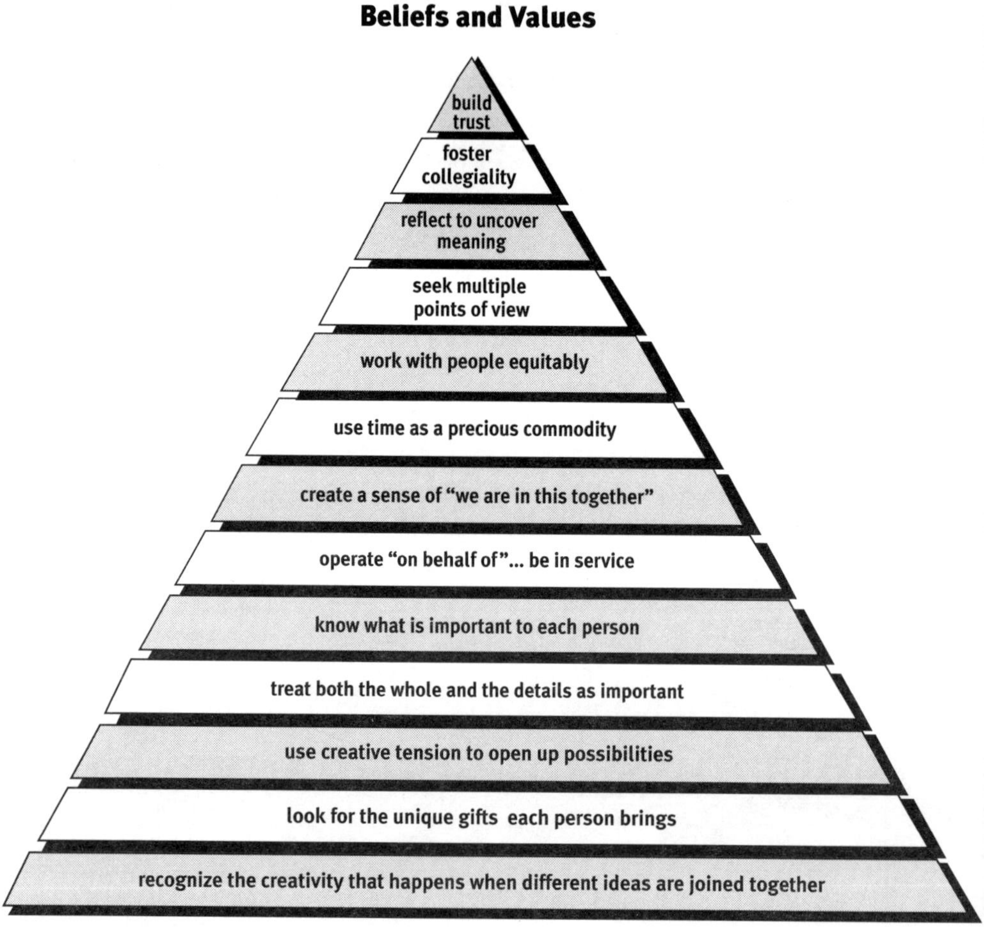

Beliefs and Values

build
trust

foster
collegiality

reflect to uncover
meaning

seek multiple
points of view

work with people equitably

use time as a precious commodity

create a sense of "we are in this together"

operate "on behalf of"... be in service

know what is important to each person

treat both the whole and the details as important

use creative tension to open up possibilities

look for the unique gifts each person brings

recognize the creativity that happens when different ideas are joined together

Figure 4

Something new emerges from thinking together based on shared values, as we think beyond the immediate and move to action.

Think with Foresight

"If it is to be, it is up to me."
– Anonymous

Today, we are all self-employed. Our job is to add value to what the organization is seeking to do in our day-to-day capacity. "Job security is earned by market success," commented a CEO in one of TeamTech's seminars, "because when we make our company successful, benefits can be there for everyone." This is a message that has been difficult to hear. Nobody has wanted to come face to face with the fact that company loyalty alone does not equate with the organization taking care of you. The paternal relationship is dead. When this message is heard loud and clear, people have the chance to move forward, take charge and think with foresight.

Encourage People to Learn

Learning is a lifelong process and facilitative leaders become guides who encourage that process in themselves and others.

- Encourage people to risk expressing their ideas. Organizations need fresh ideas and multiple points of view, not stale opinions.
  How do you make that happen? *We believe you tutor people in how to be reflective learners.*
- Encourage people to learn how to dialogue about the issues rather than defend their opinions. Organizations need people who can work smarter, not harder.
  How do you make that happen? *We believe you tutor people in how to work together.*
- Encourage people to hear what is really being said, rather than what they thought was being said. Organizations need people talking with, not at, each other.
  How do you make that happen? *We believe you tutor people in how to ask questions and listen.*
- Encourage people to learn how to take the right actions at the right time. Organizations need to be right the first time.
  How do you make that happen? *We believe you tutor people at all levels in how to think with foresight.*

When you decide to be facilitative, choose to lead and operate with a thinking style that is:

Comprehensive in outlook. This outlook anticipates change and develops a big-picture perspective as a way to discover inter-relationships and gain leverage.

Facilitative in approach. This approach recognizes that people learn by reflection, work from questions more than answers, and understand that knowledge can come from the way we think and act together to get the job done.

Intentional in actions. These actions commit to building trust, attending to details, and working to achieve alignment and consistency for people trying to work together.

Enthusiastic in imagination. This imagination employs all your skills and knowledge. You are willing to work outside your comfort zone.

Learning to be facilitative and strategic is a continuous journey.

The ancient Hindu image of the four phases of life is a metaphor for the facilitative journey in our work life. In the first phase you are an apprentice exploring ways to work with others, experiencing new methods and techniques. In the second phase you become more adventurous – creating structures and risking new avenues and approaches. With experience, by the third phase, you become the guardian of effective ways of doing things – ensuring stability in the midst of innovation. Finally, in the fourth phase, you develop reflective wisdom with new levels of objectivity and humor.

The quality of engagement changes in each phase, while continuous involvement with others keeps you on the journey even when the way seems long, uncertain or there are unexpected forks in the road.

Brother Leo:	"What are we going to do on this journey?"
Francis:	"We're going to start with small easy things – then little by little we shall try our hand at the big things – and after that – after we finish the big things, we shall undertake the impossible!"
Brother Leo:	"Undertake the impossible? What do you mean? How far do we plan to go?
Francis:	"As far as we possibly can – and then we are going to go farther than we can!"

St. Francis of Assisi, Nikos Kazantzakis[6]

End Notes

Make a Difference

1. Curt Coffman and Gabriel Gonzalez-Molina. *Follow This Path* (New York: Warner Books, 2002), p. 137.

2. Frederick Herberg. "One more time: How do you motivate employees?" Reprint from *Harvard Business Review Classic* (January-February, 1968), No. 87507.

3. Wm. Van Dusen Wishard, President, WorldTrends Research. "A New Frame of Reference," speech delivered before the Commandant and Senior Offices, United States Marine Corps, Quantico, Virginia, October 20, 1994.

4. Peter Senge, Art Kleiner, Charlotte Roberts, George Roth, Rick Ross and Bryan Smith. *The Dance of Change: The Challenges to Sustaining Momentum in Learning Organizations* (New York: Doubleday, March, 1999), p. 12.

5. Jeffrey Pfeffer and Robert Sutton. "The Smart-Talk Trap." *Harvard Business Review* (May-June, 1999), p. 135.

6. Peter Drucker. "Managing Oneself." *Harvard Business Review* (March-April, 1999), p. 71.

7. Susan Caminiti. "What Team Leaders Need to Know." *Fortune.* (February 20, 1995). www.fortune.com/fortune/print/0,15935,378681,00.html.

8. David Perkins. *Outsmarting IQ, the Emerging Science of Learnable Intelligence* (New York: Simon & Shuster, 1995), pp. 282-283.

Mobilize Energy

1. Chris Argyris. "Empowerment: The Emperor's New Clothes." *Harvard Business Review* (May-June 1998), p. 99.

2. P. Ranganth Nayak and John M. Ketteringham. *Break-throughs!* (New York: Rawson Associates, 1986), pp. 55-56.

3. James C. Collins and Jerry I. Porras. *Built to Last, Successful Habits of Visionary Companies* (New York: Harper Business, 1994), p. 159.

4. Thomas J. Peters, Robert H. Waterman, John Nathan and Sam Tyler. *In Search of Excellence* (Waltham, MA: Nathan/Tyler Productions, 1985).

5. John P. Schuster, Jill Carpenter and Patricia Kane. *The Power of Open-Book Management* (New York: John Wiley & Sons, 1996), pp. 32-34.

6. James C. Collins and Jerry I. Porras. *Built to Last, Successful Habits of Visionary Companies* (New York: Harper Collins Publishing, 1994), p. 145.

7. ibid., p. 47.

8. Basil Sharp. *The Adventure of Being Human* (Washington, DC: Integrated Life Architects, 2000), p. 135.

9. Peter Drucker. "The Theory of the Business." *Harvard Business Review* (September-October, 1994), p. 99.

10. Ikujiro Nonaka. "The Knowledge-Creating Company." *Harvard Business Review* (November-December, 1991), p. 103.

11. Peter Senge. *Fifth Discipline* (New York: Doubleday, 1990), p. 72.

12. Margaret Wheatley. *Leadership and the New Science* (San Francisco: Berrett-Koehler Publishers, Inc., 1999), p. 110.

13. Gerald Nadler and Shozo Hibino. *Breakthrough Thinking* (Sacramento, CA: Prima Publishing and Communication, 1990), p. 163.

Orchestrate Interactions

1. Paul Tillich. *The Courage to Be* (Clinton, MA: Yale University Press, 1952), p. 177.

2. Peter Block. "Redefining Accountability." *Leadership in Action* (Volume 20, No. 6, 2001), pp. 10-11.

3. Kathleen Harnish. President, TeamTech Inc. Conversation during internship with Dr. Deming, 1991.

4. Basil Sharp. *The Adventure of Being Human, A Guide to Living a Fuller Life* (Washington, DC: Integrated Life Architects, 2000), p. 127.

Generate Reflection

1. John Heider. *The Tao of Leadership, Leadership Strategies for a New Age* (New York: Bantam Books, 1985), p. 23.

2. Alan Webber. "What's So New About the New Economy." *Harvard Business Review* (January-February, 1993), p. 24.

3. Alan Webber. "Surviving in the New Economy." *Harvard Business Review* (September-October, 1994), p. 88.

4. David Bohm and F. David Peat. *Science, Order, and Creativity* (New York: Bantam Books, 1987), pp. 245-246.

5. Anthony de Mello. *Taking Flight* (New York: Image Books, Doubleday, 1990), p. 40.

6. Kaze Gadway. "The Brain's Thinking Process." Written for TeamTech, Inc., 1999.

7. Peter Drucker. "The New Society of Organizations." *Harvard Business Review* (September-October, 1992), p. 95.

8. Peter Drucker. "The Coming of the New Organization." *Harvard Business Review* (January-February, 1988), p. 49.

9. Patrick Miller. "Righting the Educational Conveyor Belt" (Washington, DC: *NEA Publication*, 1981), chapter 8, p. 1.

10. Wm. Van Dusen Wishard, President, WorldTrends Research. "A New Frame of Reference." Speech delivered before the Commandant and Senior Officers, United States Marine Corps, Quantico, Virginia, October 20, 1994.

11. Eric Jensen. *Teaching with the Brain in Mind* (Alexandria, VA: Association for Supervision and Curriculum Development, 1998), p. 95.

12. Tom Peters. *The Tom Peters Seminar* (New York: Random House, 1994), p. 12.

13. *Teaching and the Human Brain* (Alexandria, VA: Association for Supervision and Curriculum Development, 1991), p. 92.

14. ICA, Canada (Institute of Cultural Affairs), Historical Scan, Facilitation Skills Training Catalog, 2002.

15. Paula M. Diller. Retrieved from GRP-FACL@listserv.albany.edu. February 7, 2003.

16. Thomas L. Friedman. "Tone it Down a Notch." *New York Times* (Oct 2, 2002), Section A, p. 27.

Ignite Action

1. Jeffrey Pfeffer and Robert I. Sutton. "The Smart-Talk Trap." *Harvard Business Review* (May-June, 1999), p. 135.

2. ibid., p. 141.

3. Alan Webber. "Surviving in the New Economy." *Harvard Business Review* (September-October, 1994), p. 91.

4. Robert Fritz. *The Path of Least Resistance* (Salem, MA: DMA, Inc. 1984), p. 54.

5. Basil Sharp. *The Adventure of Being Human* (Washington, DC: Integrated Life Architects, 2000), p. 139.

6. Peter Drucker. "The Discipline of Innovation." *Harvard Business Review* (November-December 1998), p. 154.

7. Tehyi Hsieh. *Chinese Epigrams Inside Out and Proverbs* (New York: Exposition Press, 1948), p. 1.

8. Jon Jenkins. *International Facilitator's Companion, The Basic Workshop Method* (Groningen, The Netherlands: Imaginal Training, 1996), p. 2.

9. Brian Stanfield. *The Workshop Book* (Gabriola Island, BC, Canada: New Society Publishers, 2002), pp. 1-158.

10. Robert J. Kriegel and Louis Patler. *If It Ain't Broke, Break It!* (New York: Warner Books, Inc., 1991), p. 13.

11. Lewis Carroll. *The Annotated Alice: Alice's Adventures in Wonderland* (New York: Random House, 1960), p. 88.

12. Santo Cilauro and Tom Gleisner. Rob Sitch, Director. *The Dish* (Burbank, CA: Warner Home Video), 2001.

Capture Learning

1. Peter Senge. *The Fifth Discipline* (New York: Bantam Doubleday Dell Publishing Group, 1990), p. 14.

2. Jerry I. Prosser and James C. Collins. *Built to Last* (New York: Harper Collins, 1994), pp. 80-90.

3. Alvin Toffler. *Future Shock* (New York: Random House, 1970), p. 356.

4. "Groupthink." CRM Learning Video (Carlsbad, CA: CRM Producer and Director, 1990).

5. David Perkins. *Outsmarting IQ, The Emerging Science of Learnable Intelligence* (New York: The Free Press, Division of Simon & Schuster, 1995), pp. 160-162.

6. Daniel Yankelovich, Interview with Bill Moyer. NOW, PBS, June 14, 2002.

7. Kaze Gadway. Gadway Associates, *Transfer Training*. Adapted from the work of Michael Grinder & Associates for TeamTech Inc., 1999.

8. ibid., p. 2

9. ibid., p. 3

10. Leslie Wayne and Leslie Kaufman. "Leadership Put to the Test – a Response to This Crisis Couldn't Be Learned in an M.B.A. Class." *The New York Times* (September 16, 2001), p. BU1 – Col. 3.

11. "Everyone A Leader"®, TeamTech, Inc. Trademark, Department of Commerce, 1995.

12. "Hot Topic for Executives." *USA Today Snapshots, USA TODAY* (June 26, 2002), p. 1.

13. Rolf Jensen. *The Dream Society: How the Coming Shift From Information to Imagination will Transform Your Business* (Columbus, OH: McGraw-Hill, 1999), pp. 36-50.

14. Peter Senge. *The Fifth Discipline Fieldbook* (New York: Doubleday, 1994), p. 89.

15. Peter Senge. "Why Organizations Still Aren't Learning." *Training* (September 1999), p. 46.

What It Takes

1. "Everyone A Leader"®, TeamTech, Inc. Trademark, Department of Commerce, 1995.

2. Jon and Maureen Jenkins. "The Personal Disciplines of a Facilitator." International Association of Facilitators Conference, Ft. Worth, TX, May, 2002.

3. Peter Block. *The Answer to How Is Yes* (San Francisco: Berrett-Koehler Publishers, Inc., 2002), p. 127.

4. Gregory S. Berns. "Why We're So Nice: We're Wired to Cooperate." *The New York Times, Science Times* (July 23, 2002), p. F1.

5. Jo Nelson and Brian Stanfield. Ten Rules of Order for Century XXI, Clashing Images of Participation, *EDGES* (August, 2000). Permission to use in email, September 24, 2002.

6. Nikos Kazantzakis. *Saint Francis* (New York: Simon & Shuster, 1962), p. 63.

Suggested Readings – Books

Adams, John D. (General Editor). *Transforming Work*. Alexandria, VA: Miles River Press, 1984.

Adams, John D. (General Editor). *Transforming Leadership*. Alexandria, VA: Miles River Press, 1986.

Bennis, Warren. *On Becoming a Leader*. Reading, MA: Addison-Wesley Publishing Company, 1989.

Block, Peter. *The Answer to How Is Yes*. San Francisco: Berrett-Koehler Publishers, Inc., 2002.

Block, Peter. *Stewardship*. San Francisco: Berrett-Koehler Publishers, Inc., 1993.

Bolman, Lee G. and Deal, Terrence E. *Reframing Organizations*. San Francisco: Jossey-Bass Publications, 1991.

Bohm, David and Peat, F. David. *Science, Order, and Creativity*. New York: Bantam Books, 1987.

Byham, William. *Zapp! The Lightening of Empowerment*. New York: Ballantine Books, 1988.

Campbell, Susan. *From Chaos to Confidence, Survival Strategies for the New Workplace*. New York: Simon & Schuster, 1995.

Collins, James C. and Porras, Jerry I. *Built to Last*. New York: HarperBusiness, 1994.

Deal, Terrence E. and Kennedy, Allan A. *Corporate Cultures, The Rites and Rituals of Corporate Life*. Reading, MA: Addison-Wesley Publishing Company, 1982.

Fritz, Robert. *The Path of Least Resistance*. Salem, MA: DMA Inc., 1984.

Fritz, Robert. *Creating*. New York: Ballantine Books, 1991.

Geus, Arie de. *The Living Company.* Boston, MA: Harvard Business School Press, 1997.

Heider, John. *The Tao of Leadership, Leadership Strategies for a New Age.* New York: Bantam Books, 1985.

Jaworski, Joseph. *Synchronicity, The Inner Path of Leadership.* San Francisco: Berrett-Koehler Publishers, Inc., 1996.

Jenkins, Jon and Jenkins, Maureen. *International Facilitator's Companion.* Groningen, The Netherlands: Imaginal Training, 1996.

Jenkins, Jon and Jenkins, Maureen. *The Social Process Triangles.* Groningen, The Netherlands: Imaginal Training, 1997.

Jensen, Rolf. *The Dream Society: How the Coming Shift From Information to Imagination Will Transform Your Business.* Columbus, OH: McGraw-Hill, 1999.

Kanter, Rosabeth Moss. *Change Masters.* New York: Simon & Shuster, 1983.

Kazantzakis, Nikos. *Saint Francis.* New York: Simon & Shuster, 1962.

Kegan, Robert and Lahey, Lisa Laskow. *How the Way We Talk Can Change the Way We Work.* San Francisco: Jossey-Bass, 2001.

Kouzes, James and Posner, Barry. *The Leadership Challenge.* San Francisco: Jossey-Bass, Inc., 1987.

Kriegel, Robert J. and Patler, Louis. *If It Ain't Broke, BREAK IT!* New York: Warner Books, Inc., 1991.

McLagan, Patricia and Nel, Christo. *The Age of Participation.* San Francisco: Berrett-Koehler Publishers, Inc., 1995.

Nadler, Gerald and Hibino, Shozo. *Breakthrough Thinking.* Sacramento, CA: Prima Publishing and Communication, 1990.

Nayak, Ranganth P. and Ketteringham, John M. *Break-throughs!* New York: Rawson Associates, 1986.

Perkins, David. *Outsmarting IQ, The Emerging Science of Learnable Intelligence.* New York: Simon & Schuster, 1995.

Peters, Tom. *The Pursuit of WOW!* New York: Vintage Books, 1994.

Peters, Tom. *Thriving on Chaos.* New York: HarperPerennial, 1987.

Peters, Tom. *The Tom Peters Seminar.* New York: Random House, 1994.

Russell, Peter and Evans, Roger. *The Creative Manager.* San Francisco: Jossey-Bass, Inc., 1992.

Schuster, John P., Carpenter, Jill and Kane, Patricia. *The Power of Open-Book Management.* New York: John Wiley & Sons, 1996.

Senge, Peter M. *The Fifth Discipline.* New York: Doubleday, 1990.

Senge, Peter M. *The Fifth Discipline Fieldbook.* New York: Doubleday, 1994.

Senge, Peter M., Kleiner, Art, Roberts, Charlotte, Roth, George, Ross, Rick and Smith, Bryan. *The Dance of Change: The Challenges to Sustaining Momentum in Learning Organizations.* New York: Doubleday, 1999.

Sharp, Basil. *The Adventure of Being Human.* Washington, DC: Integrated Life Architects, 2000.

Spencer, Laura. *Winning Through Participation.* Dubuque, IA: Kendall/Hunt Publishing Company, 1989.

Stanfield, Brian R. (Editor). *The Art of Focused Conversation.* Toronto, Canada: The Canadian Institute of Cultural Affairs, 1997.

Stanfield, Brian R. *The Courage to Lead.* Gabriola Island, BC, Canada: New Society Publishers, 2000.

Stanfield, Brian R. *The Workshop Book, from Individual Creativity to Group Action.* Gabriola Island, BC, Canada: New Society Publishers, 2002.

Tillich, Paul. *The Courage to Be.* Clinton, MA: Yale University Press, 1952.

Wheatley, Margaret. *Leadership and the New Science.* San Francisco: Berrett-Koehler Publishers, Inc., 1992.

Williams, R. Bruce. *More Than 50 Ways to Build Team Consensus.* Arlington Heights, IL: IRI/Skylight Training and Publishing, Inc., 1993.

Suggested Readings – Articles

Argyris, Chris. "Good Communication That Blocks Learning." *Harvard Business Review* (July-August, 1994), pp. 77-85.

Caminiti, Susan. "What Team Leaders Need to Know." *Fortune* (February 20, 1995), www.fortune.com/fortune/print/0,15935,378681,00.html.

Drucker, Peter. "The Coming of the New Organization." *Harvard Business Review* (January-February, 1988), pp. 45-53.

Drucker, Peter. "Managing Oneself." *Harvard Business Review* (March-April, 1999), pp. 64-74.

Drucker, Peter F. "The New Productivity Challenge." *Harvard Business Review* (November-December, 1991), pp. 69-79.

Garvin, David A. "Building a Learning Organization." *Harvard Business Review* (July-August, 1993), pp. 78-91.

Herzberg, Frederick. "One more time: How do you motivate employees?" *Harvard Business Review Classic.* Reprinted from *Harvard Business Review* (No. 87507), pp. 1-9.

Isaacs, William N. "Taking Flight: Dialogue, Collective Thinking, and Organizational Learning." *Organizational Dynamics* (Autumn, 1993), pp. 24-39.

Kanter, Rosabeth Moss. "The New Managerial Work." *Harvard Business Review* (November-December, 1989), pp. 85-92.

Peters, Tom. "Selling Imagination." *Edges* (Winter, 1994, Vol. 6, No. 1), pp. 13-15.

Pfeffer, Jeffrey and Sutton, Robert I. "The Smart-Talk Trap." *Harvard Business Review* (May-June, 1999), pp. 134-142.

Senge, Peter. "The Leader's New Work: Building Learning Organizations." *Sloan Management Review, Reprint Series* (Fall 1990, Volume 32, Number 1), pp. 7-23.

Senge, Peter. "Why Organizations Still Aren't Learning." *Training* (September, 1999), pp. 40-49.

Stewart, Thomas A. "Intellectual Capital." *Fortune* (October 3, 1994, Vol. 130, Issue 7), pp. 68-74.

Stewart, Thomas A. "Brain Power, Who Owns It, How They Profit From It." *Fortune* (March 17, 1997, Vol. 135, Issue 5), pp. 104-109.

Webber, Alan M. "What's So New About the New Economy." *Harvard Business Review* (January-February, 1993), No. 93109, pp. 4-12.

Appendix

History of the Dynamics Screen

In the mid-1960s the Ecumenical Institute of Chicago conducted research in a westside Chicago community. The early research included a door-to-door survey of the problems of the community. As these hundreds of problems were analyzed, "a set of models began to be developed that would allow individuals to look at all of human experience from a complex but easily understood perspective."[1] This work on defining the social process was further pursued in a global reading research project.

In the fall of 1970, "1,500 books were studied and reported on by the staff and volunteers in dozens of locations around the world. This Corporate Reading Research Project was followed up by a research team that varied in size and composition around a core of 30 people every weekend during the winter and spring of 1971. In the summer of 1971 some 1,500 people came to Chicago and participated in a research project aimed at using the social processes to discern the issues facing global society."[2] This resulted in the development of a triangular picture of the dynamics of any society, the Social Process Screen. The construction of the Social Process Screen included the following values:

- inclusive – to examine social dynamics throughout history in all societies and hold traditional wisdom,
- consistent – to describe the dynamical relationships between people and their environment,
- comprehensive – to leave no dynamics out of the model and to illustrate in an imaginal way the dynamical relationships in any organizational reality.

For the past thirty years, the Social Process Dynamics model has been used by the Institute of Cultural Affairs, a branch of the Ecumenical Institute, globally to solve problems and heighten understanding in corporate boardrooms as well as rural villages. It has been used as a diagnostic tool in analysis as well as a strategizing tool for planning and projecting the future. This screen was adapted as a tool for the business community in the 1980s.

In the 1990s, TeamTech, Inc., working with the original research, repositioned the Dynamics Screen as a user-friendly tool for corporate, governmental and non-profit organizations to use to:

- be comprehensive in analyzing a situation
- identify trends and patterns to determine where to focus energy
- discover strategic and system leverage when deciding where to focus efforts
- build implementation strategies

1. Jon C. Jenkins and Maureen R. Jenkins. *The Social Process Triangles* (Groningen, The Netherlands: Imaginal Training 1997), p. 5.

2. ibid.

History of the Conversation Formula

R. Brian Stanfield describes the birth of the reflective questioning formula in detail in the introduction to *The Art of Focused Conversation.* The method began in the mind of army chaplain Joseph Mathews as he pondered the failure of dialogue during World War II. Mathews connected his thinking with that of the nineteenth-century Danish philosopher Soren Kierkegaard and other twentieth-century thinkers. Experiments in the university community led to the art form conversation method, with objective, reflective, interpretive and decision questions, also known as the O-R-I-D method. This method became a foundation of the ICA (Institute of Cultural Affairs) community-building efforts around the world. Brian Stanfield worked with this method for many years as an ICA staff member. It was first described in published material by Laura Spencer in *Winning Through Participation.*

TeamTech, Inc. modified the language of sequencing questions to FFID (facts, feelings, implications, decision) for more ease of use in the language. This question sequence formula follows the natural thinking process in the original method: facts, objective data – feelings, reflection on experience – implications, interpretation – decision.

History of the Workshop Method

The Workshop Method was created by the Institute of Cultural Affairs as a tool for eliciting community participation in problem-solving. This context-brainstorming-organizing-naming method picked up on the brainstorming method heavily in vogue in the United States in the 1950s and 1960s and combined it with the process from gestalt psychology created by the Germans Wertheimer, Kohler and Koffka.

In the 1980s the Workshop Method was used extensively in the Institute's training and planning programs. The method was moulded to follow the same underlying pattern as the artform conversation: objective, reflective, interpretive, and decisional.

In the 1990s, TeamTech further defined the method by reframing the Categorizing, Naming and Action Steps to enable clients to more easily move brainstorm ideas to action. Brian Stanfield's work in *The Workshop Book, From Individual Creativity to Group Action* further outlines the history of this method.

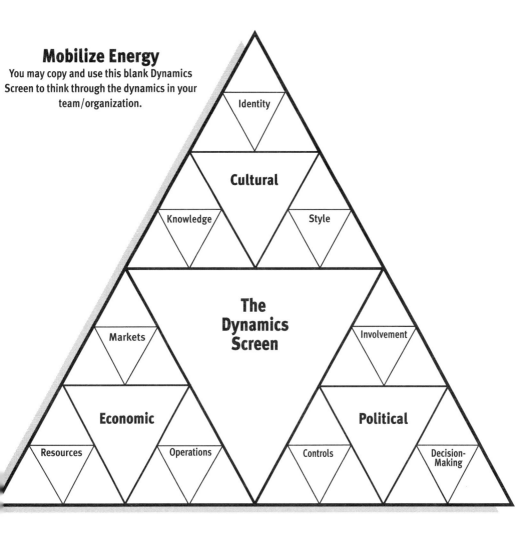

Mobilize Energy

You may copy and use this blank Dynamics Screen to think through the dynamics in your team/organization.

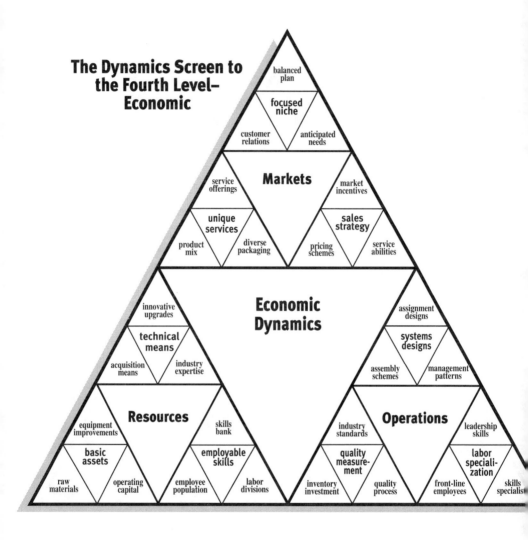

The Dynamics Screen to the Fourth Level–Economic

The Dynamics Screen to the Fourth Level
Further definition of the dynamics – Economic, Political and Cultural –
to assist in your thinking.

The Dynamics Screen to the Fourth Level– Political

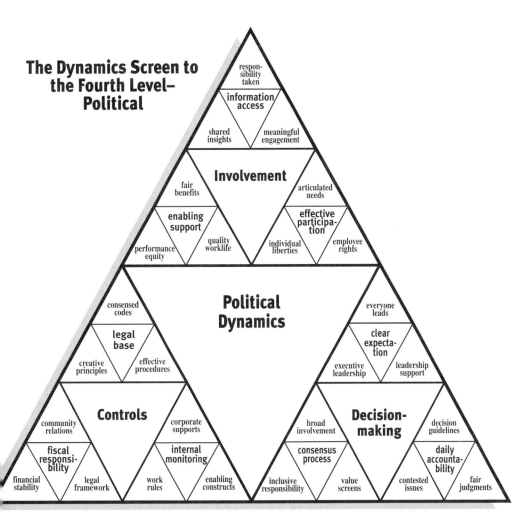

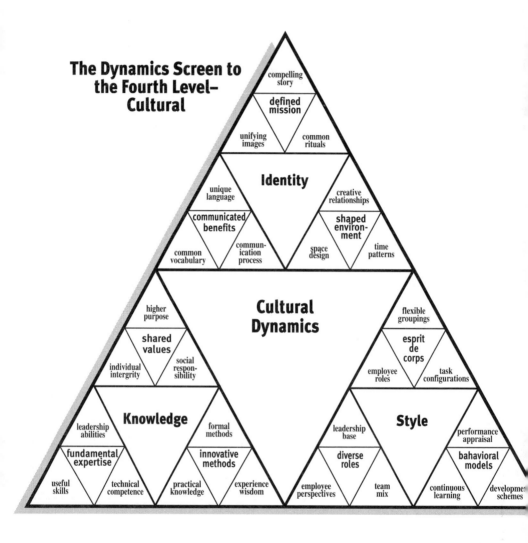

The Dynamics Screen to the Fourth Level– Cultural

compelling story

defined mission

unifying images

common rituals

Identity

unique language

creative relationships

communicated benefits

shaped environ- ment

common vocabulary

commun- ication process

space design

time patterns

Cultural Dynamics

higher purpose

flexible groupings

shared values

esprit de corps

individual intergrity

social respon- sibility

employee roles

task configurations

Knowledge

Style

leadership abilities

formal methods

leadership base

performance appraisal

fundamental expertise

innovative methods

diverse roles

bahavioral models

useful skills

technical competence

practical knowledge

experience wisdom

employee perspectives

team mix

continuous learning

developme schemes

Conversation Practice

Situation:_____

Kinds of questions	Questions I can ask	Listening for
Facts • get the facts • what see, hear? • who involved? • when, where?		specificity in facts and data
Feelings • like/dislike? • similar experiences?		associations, feelings, previous experiences
Implications •important? • what mean? • will change?		meaning, point of view, values, common arenas
Decision • what's been said? • need to do now? • what's next?		resolve, commitment, responsibility, decision

You may copy this chart in order to practice writing out questions
for a particular situation.

Sample Conversations

Teams
Intent: To know what it is like to be on a team. To experience the excitement of being a member of a team.

Context: We get assigned to a team for this ... or for that ... and often we're not sure what that will mean. I thought it would be helpful to take a few minutes this afternoon to think about what being on a team means for us.

Facts:
1. What is the first thing you think of when you hear the word "team"?
2. What famous team can you think of ... besides a sports team?

Feelings:
3. What is a team you've been on in your lifetime ... that you were proud of?

Implications:
4. People often say a team "jells"... what do they mean?
5. How has being on a team cared for you ... what happened to you?

Decision:
6. Why is there so much emphasis on "team" today?

Closing: "Teams" are something we all are familiar with, and yet we continually need to think together to figure out how to be one here at work.

Opportunity
Intent: To know when opportunity is knocking on our door. To experience excitement about the opportunities that come day-to-day.

Context: We all have many opportunities. Sometimes we recognize them and at other times we miss them. Let's take a few minutes to talk together about what "opportunity" looks like for us.

Facts:
1.   Name one opportunity that you have been aware of.

Feelings:
2.   What did your opportunity feel like?

Implications:
3.   What is something that has happened to you because of opportunity?
4.   What are opportunities that are knocking on the door for you now?

Decision:
5.   What is one piece of advice you would give to someone else about "opportunity"?

Closing: Opportunities appear every day. Maybe we can help each other take advantage of the opportunities that will make our day-to-day work less complicated.

Quality Service Providers

Intent: To know what quality service looks like. To experience the pleasure of being a quality service provider.

Context: Too often "quality" becomes a separate program as opposed to something we are involved in all the time. I thought it would be helpful if we shared some of our experiences in providing quality in our day-to-day work.

Facts:
1.   What is one thing you think of when you hear the term "quality service"?
2.   Where do you interface with our clients ... at what points in our service?

Feelings:
3.   What are occasions that are likely to cause a client to think ... "I received excellent (or poor) treatment?"

Implications:

4. Where are there real opportunities to provide quality service in our day-to-day work?

Decision:

5. What will count with clients the most in the future?

Closing: Thank you for taking the time to think about our relationship with our clients.

Leadership

Intent: To know what it means to be a leader. To experience the excitement of providing leadership where we are in our job.

Context: We think of "promoted" or "assigned" people as those who are leaders, and yet we know that each of us is a leader in many ways. Let's think a few minutes about what that means in our day-to-day situations.

Facts:

1. What is one picture that comes to mind when you hear the word "leadership"?

Feelings:

2. What leaders do you think of ... world, nation, community, this organization?
3. What qualities do these people have that make them leaders?

Implications:

4. What is the key to providing leadership in a given situation?

Decision:

5. How will you develop your own leadership capabilities?

Closing: It is helpful to remind ourselves that we are each leaders wherever we are. Thank you for taking the time to think about what that means for us.

Working Environment

Intent: To consider how space and sound create maximum productivity. To experience that we shape our working environment.

Context: We've all experienced different working spaces. I thought it might be helpful to share what works well in our work environment ... and what doesn't.

Facts:
1. When you think of your working environment, what is the first image (picture) that comes to your mind?

Feelings:
2. What about your working space helps you the most? hinders you the most?

Implications:
3. What have you discovered makes the most difference in your working environment and why? arrangement of furniture, walls, noise, proximity of people.

Decision:
4. What can you do to ensure an effective working environment?

Closing: Sometimes we think we have no control over our space ... until we stop and look around and realize we can do a lot with what we have.

Trust

Intent: To acknowledge the ambiguity of the word "trust." To experience that trust begins with us.

Context: "Trust" is a word that we hear people talk about a lot. Let's take a few minutes to examine "trust" and see what we are thinking.

Facts:
1. What do you think of when you hear the word "trust"?

Feelings:
2.   How does it feel when you are in an organization, relationship, team where there is trust?
3.   When there is no trust?

Implications:
4.   What are the things that create trust? Where does it come from?

Decision:
5.   What are things you can do in your workplace to ensure trust is present?

Closing: Trust is not something we work on directly. It is very much a by-product of all the ways we work with each other.

Review of the Day
Intent: To recapture what has gone on during the day. To experience that the day was "good."

Context: Whenever we are part of an event or participate in an activity, it is helpful to stop and reflect on what we did. Let's take a few minutes before we close the day to recall what we have been doing.

Facts:
1.   What is one thing you remember that happened today ... you did, one of your colleagues did, an activity, etc.?
2.   What did someone say that is still in your mind?

Feelings:
3.   Which activities seemed most on target for you?
4.   Which activities were not as helpful for you?

Implications:
5. What was the most important learning for you?
6. What difference will what we did today make in your workplace during the coming days/weeks?

Decision:
7. What do you intend to do to "practice" the things that you have learned?

Closing: We each experience an event in a different way. It is always useful to hear what happened to other people as well as to recall what happened to us.

About the Authors

Trained as an educator and retired from TeamTech, Inc., **Priscilla H. Wilson** has spent thirty-five years training groups and individuals to communicate and work effectively together. Her work as a program designer, curriculum creator and trainer for leaders and facilitators has taken her across North America, South America, Pacific Islands, Northeast Asia and Europe. Priscilla has worked with governmental, community and non-profit organizations, as well as corporate businesses.

She led the youth program in a local church in the 1960s, which enabled teenagers to study life issues and communication challenges. Priscilla trained suburban women in diversity issues and life skills when working with an inner-city community development project in the Chicago area. She designed curriculum and training packages for church lay committees to use in "renewing the church" across the USA in the 1970s.

Priscilla worked with the Institute of Cultural Affairs (ICA) as a program designer and facilitator. She was one of a group of designers for the Global Women's Forum and LENS (Leadership Effectiveness and New Strategies). Each of these program was conducted on six continents. Priscilla served as an ICA board member for fifteen years.

Priscilla served on the staff of the Pacific Training School in Tonga in 1983. While there, she designed and facilitated curriculum to train men and women to work together to create and implement development plans for that island nation. Priscilla trained eighteen facilitators to work with small groups in the Symposium on Needs Assessment held by The Women's Foundation of Greater Kansas City in May, 1992. She served as a table facilitator in the July, 2002, Listening to the City town meeting. Sponsored by the Civic Alliance to Rebuild Downtown New York, this event facilitated local input on the future of Ground Zero.

Priscilla's expertise encompasses program development, graphic design, facilitative training and mentoring. She was awarded the Dear Neighbor Award by the Sisters of Saint Joseph of Carondelet and the Saint Joseph Health System and recognized for services to The Young Black Male Symposium by the Kansas City Missouri School District. The United Nations Kansas City

World Citizen of the Year was awarded to Priscilla in 1986. Her articles on teamwork have been published in the *Kansas City Business Journal* and *The Kansas City Star*. She earned a BA in education from the University of Oklahoma with advanced studies at Northeastern University in Chicago. Priscilla is a member of the International Association of Facilitators.

Kathleen Harnish-Doucet, CEO of TeamTech, is a respected consultant/facilitator whose twenty years of business experience include facilitation, strategic planning, team building, organizational development, training, critical process redesign, international business and investment management. Kathleen has worked nationally with clients like Southwest Securities and Financial Network Investment Corporation. She co-authored a top-selling video, *Implementing Total Quality Management*, produced and marketed by CareerTrack®. She has presented at the International Association of Facilitators Conference and, in the summer of 2002, was selected by the leaders of a local input session sponsored by the Civic Alliance to Rebuild Downtown New York to facilitate a discussion among New Yorkers on the future of Ground Zero.

Kathleen earned a bachelor's of business administration summa cum laude from Pittsburg State University and an MBA summa cum laude from the University of Kansas. Kathleen received the Chartered Financial Analyst designation in 1991 and completed an internship with Dr. W. Edwards Deming, one of the key creators and teachers of the quality management concepts. Her articles on quality management have appeared in *Securities Industry Management* and *Financial Planning News*. Kathleen is a member of the International Association of Facilitators and the American Society for Training and Development.

W. Joel Wright, vice president of TeamTech, Inc., brings thirty years of worldwide experience that has taken him from local villages to global boardrooms. He is a master facilitator with expertise in organizational development, strategic thinking, problem solving, team building and handling emotionally difficult situations. His global client list is represented by Mobil Oil, Indonesia, the Zambian Government, Africa, the Community Council, Tairgwaith Wales, Europe and the Kentucky Commerce Cabinet, USA. In 1984, he was a key facilitator of the International Exposition of Rural Developmental in New

Delhi, India, which brought together 600 local village and community people from 55 nations to share approaches that work. His current consulting/facilitation focuses primarily on healthcare, finance and government.

Joel earned a bachelor's degree from William Jewell College and a master's from St. Paul's School of Theology. He was certified in the Values in Leadership Facilitator Program by the Carondelet Health System and received the Good Neighbor Award for outstanding support and partnership by the Sisters of St. Joseph of Carondelet and the Saint Joseph Health System. He was recognized for his services to The Young Black Male Symposium by the Kansas City School District and commissioned a Kentucky Colonel for his work with the Kentucky commerce Cabinet. He was the driving force behind the initial effort that produced *Winning Through Participation*, a best-selling book that shares basic facilitation skills and techniques. He has written a series of articles on leadership for the Kansas Business Report of the *Topeka Capital Journal.*

The Facilitative Way
Leadership That Makes the Difference
Feedback

As you work to be more facilitative and operate strategically, we would like your feedback.

Experience:
Is *The Facilitative Way* user friendly?

> Yes . . . Please note why.

> No . . . What would make it more user friendly?

Learnings:
What is one way you have used *The Facilitative Way?*

What have you learned?

What new things have you been able to do because of it?

Successful Applications:

Share one or two new methods or strategies you have created to help people work together effectively.

Your name:

Address:

Phone number:

Fax number:

E-mail:

Return to: TeamTech Press, 3215 Tomahawk Rd., Shawnee Mission, KS 66208
E-mail: pwilson@teamtechinc.com

The Facilitative Way
Leadership That Makes the Difference
Priscilla H. Wilson
Kathleen Harnish and Joel Wright

To order your copy, fill out this order form and
send to the address below.

Name

Company

Address

City/State/Zip

Phone Number   E-mail

Price per copy	**$24.95**
Quantity ordered	
Subtotal	
Sales tax*	**6.40%**
Shipping and handling**	
Total	

*Please add Kansas sales tax of 6.40% for books
shipped to Kansas addresses.
**Please add $4.00 per book for shipping and handling.
Allow 30 days for delivery.
Full payment must accompany your order.
Prices subject to change without notice.

Quantity orders invited. Please write for bulk account prices.

Make checks payable to:

TeamTech Press
3215 Tomahawk Rd., Shawnee Mission, KS 66208

Index

The Facilitative Way

The Facilitative Way

The Facilitative Way

The Facilitative Way